FACES TO THE SUN

A MENTAL HEALTH ANTHOLOGY

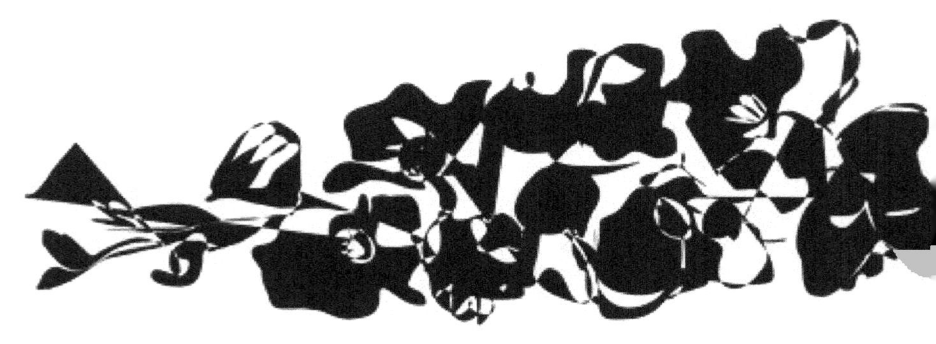

Contributors

Becky B.
Sarah Birch
SJ Blasko
Maggie D. Brace
Maggie Chang
Jackie Chou
Riley M Courtney
Jessica Critcher
Lucinda Cylights
Erelah Emerson
Ojo Olumide Emmanuel
Adrien Farinas
Margaret Ferreira
Beka Gremikova
Cassandra Hamm
Katie Hanna
Sarah Hindmarsh
Eddie L. House
Kalandfitz
Kath Kane
Naomi Karsudjono
Suzanne Lea
Polina Litvak
Angelina Luo
Nathaniel Luscombe

Amanda McCoy

S. Rupsha Mitra

Guna Moran

Karen R. Nelson

OJR

Theo Oliver

Erik Olson

Somjeeta Pandey

Frey Pokorny

Kimmy Renee

Naomi Slingerland

Stardust

Stephanie Stone

R. Sunshine

Tiberius

Martina Weiß

Noelle Weymouth

Lynn White

Clover Zicolella

Ziel

Table of Contents

Untitled – Slingerland
Untitled – Renee
Rosemary – OJR
Dandelions – Hanna
Untitled – Emerson
Untitled – Kane
Zinnia – Pandey
I Will Never Walk That Path Again. – House
Prescribed Burning – Farinas
Untitled – Pokorny
Growing Things – Blasko
Untitled – Emerson
Untitled – Zicolella

Part X: For You//To Be Loved
Gaia – Sunshine
Untitled – Emerson
the noose – Hamm
Untitled – Stardust
let's be sunflowers – Renee
Untitled – McCoy
Untitled – OJR
Untitled – Weiß
(The lesser-known name for amaranth is just a bit more inclusive) – Emerson
Untitled – Kane
Lorna & Bryoni – McCoy
Celandine tea – Emerson
Do Not Worry – Oliver
Untitled – Emerson

The Mailman

the mailman must know I am depressed.
and if he does know, then he is the only one.
you cannot convince the mailman you're getting by when
    your mail has been piling up for months and your curtains
    are always drawn.
when your car never moves and visitors never come by.
I am waiting for the mailman to see that even the vines have
    outgrown their solace.
maybe he will send someone to look for me.
if anyone knows I am not doing well then it is the mailman.

Kath Kane

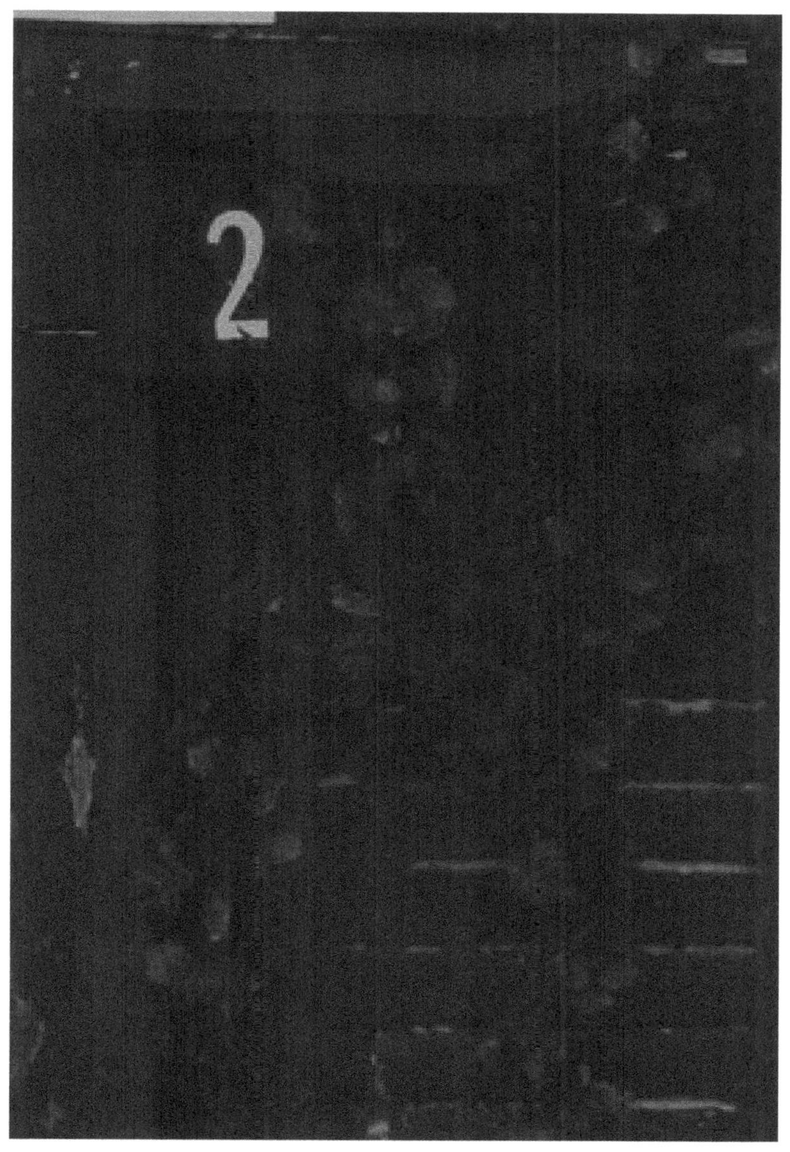

Kath Kane

FOR SAFETY//TO PROTECT

Purple anemone

for protection from evil.

Heather

in admiration,
for good luck and protection

Verbena:

for healing,
creativity,
happiness.
for protection against evil and harm.

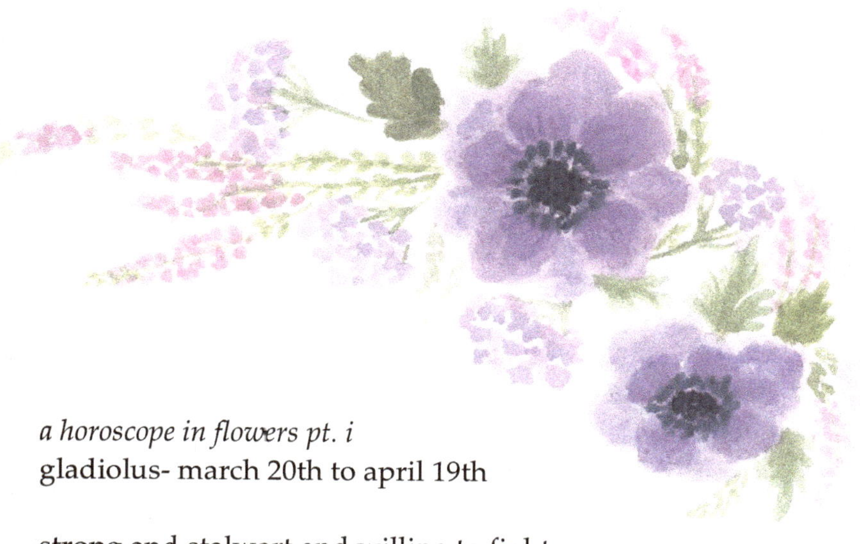

a horoscope in flowers pt. i
gladiolus- march 20th to april 19th

strong and stalwart and willing to fight
aries
lay down your weapons for the ones you love
you are bleeding
flowers sprouting from your wounds, the
gladioluses that encapsulate you so well
little weapons sprouting from your blood
but it is alright now
allow yourself to be taken care of

Your lucky numbers are 26, 43, and 10.

Signal (Facing the Sun, as the Lotus Blooms)

I have to admit
Among the things I wrangle with
One of them is trauma

Racial trauma is something I live with
A constant struggle of belonging, identity, and fighting to be
    seen,
Being in the in-between because neither Canada or China
    would accept me as I am
Too Chinese-faced to be Canadian (what even does that
    mean, this country built on stolen land, stolen dreams,
    my people used as means to accomplish that)
Too foreign valued, foreign *accustomed* to fit in, be happy,
    living in China

And now I also get to know what triggered *really* means
It is suddenly being attacked by crying
Brought back to "I, am in so much pain, and I don't know
    why"
It is sitting there, frozen, trying to stem the tide so you don't
    have to run out of class
It is angrily brushing back the tears because it's not fair, but
    you have a job interview and what will they do if you
    show up red-eyed?

This all happened because a program at my university stuck
    me in an unequal
power reality for almost a year

In some ways it seems silly it had such an impact
But maybe it's not what happened but what it represented
What it is a part of

Maybe it activated the same parts of me
That tell me to be afraid for my life
A warning cue imprinted on my DNA because
the beginning is only steps away
From experiments and cages, pages arranged in alphabetical
    order meticulously documenting slaughter
I'm not kidding the concentration camp officers
claim the Final Solution was never the plan
It began organically, ran
away from them
Because they never thought of what it would be like to be
    someone different than
them

And no matter the context
It is *painful*
when you aren't treated like a human being

--

So can you please acknowledge how *ridiculous* it is
That I had to turn on *survival switches*
To handle the circumstances you stuck me with

You should have made it start with me
I am not an externality, abnormality that you can adapt your
    white-centred approach to

That you can make adapt your white-centered approach

It's not my job
To always have to understand what you mean
So you can prance around a hero for
allowing me to exist

You took my safety, took the foundation from underneath
    my feet
My confidence, my sense of self, my ability to achieve
It was like white supremacy screaming at
me
You can be brilliant and thoughtful and kind, build yourself
    up, a clematis so tall
But I can still get you and *look* how hard you fall

You stole *my* dream
Who I used to be
Ground me down into the ground and told me I should be
    happy
I had to fight to breathe
A structural inequality *re*-placing me, backed up by violence
Do you have any idea how scary it is to have to *fight*
for the ability to exist?

And the most frightening part is
No one can ever protect me from something like this
    happening again
Because racism doesn't care *who* I am

And so now I am wounded

A hole punched through me…

How do you move on?

Because trauma works in cycles
It heals lopsided, it leaves scars
Maybe
it doesn't heal at all

Maybe…
it doesn't need to
As a brilliant person I know said to me,
Maybe all you need to do is mark the edges,
so you won't fall through
Stitch a dotted line boldly, black thread on a white shirt
Cauterize the sides so they don't fray
Lay down a
velvet rope

Because maybe the hole isn't a wound
Facing the sun, as the Lotus blooms
Maybe it's a signal
that you made it through

Maggie Chang

start from the beginning

i have a pet i think
that isn't right. let me start over.
i have a wild beast
it follows my family
howling and baring its teeth
whenever i try to mention it
it bites my arm
with fiery jaws
it almost clasped its fangs around my neck once
people politely do not mention it.
(that isn't right. let me start over.)
i am drowning with a weight attached to my ankle
when i was younger and
kinder
i used to scream to try to get people to help me
but with every scream the weight would grow heavier
and my voice would grow hoarser
until i learned that it was better not to scream at all
and just thrash and flail
hoping to make it to the surface myself
(that isn't right. let me start over.)
i am scraping my way up from a no man's land
covered in mud and blood
that might very well be mine
was, at one point, mine
the last time i asked for help
they threw me on the front lines and said find your way out
people who should have known better

and when i saw their faces again
they did not speak of what they had done to me
(that shouldn't be right. but it is.)

Adrien Farinas

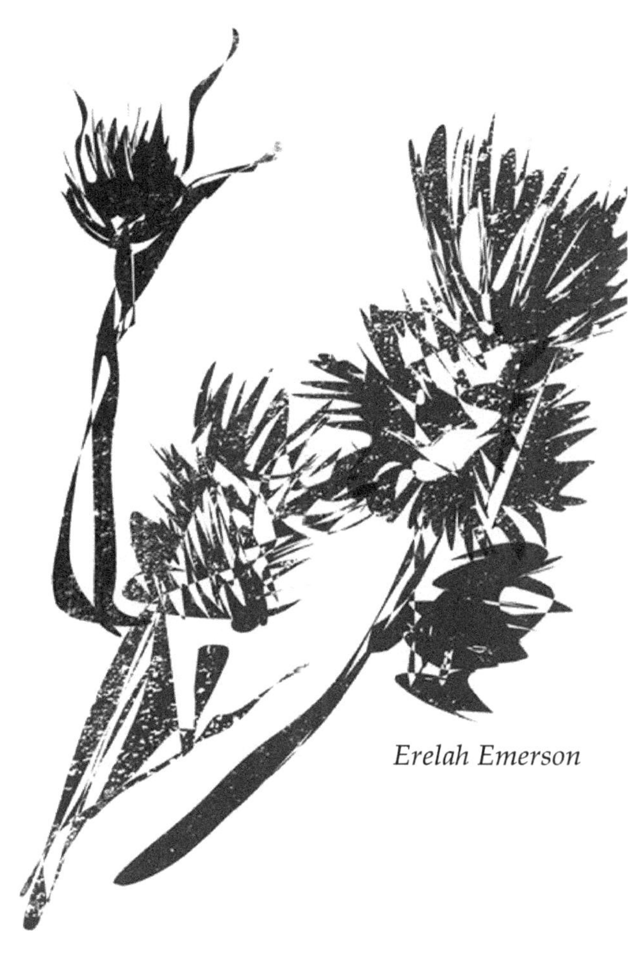

Erelah Emerson

Dandelion

Oh to be fleeing
from the common eye,
I just want to lay my head down,
though I cannot
tell you why

If I could
tell them
where I'm supposed to be

(I think you'd throw a fit)

but it's not here,
it's not with colored lenses,
no,
just not one bit,

I sit on cushioned chairs of orange,
letting leaves pass
by my sight,
but I'm not falling
with
them;
(though I wish it,)
(though I might,)

But all the black birds
with their angry beaks
that peck against the door-

are shouting
no,
no falling,
maybe, no,
you cannot reach the floor,

I look down at the place of gardens
where I will never go,
and I ask them to let me glimpse it,
I just need to know,

I say oh to be fleeing from the common eye,
there is no fleeing,
There is no falling,
There is none of that,
They cry

I watch their feathers, as they laugh,
crows privileged with a joy
that's never found me,
though I search for
anyone who knows the ploy

I look down at the place of gardens
Where they hold my tranquilizer
and I ask
why am I so bad that
I can't be fertilizer?

They mock
oh to be fleeing

from the common eye,
but they begin to chant
there is no fleeing from us
Who own
the sky

Then give my hands something to
do so I don't fret with seeing,
I tell them
this all hidden,

(I wonder if I'm being-)

I look down at the place of gardens
that I can never reach,
(I ask for just one flower
so I can wish for peace,)

I sit on such an orange chair
learning to be afraid,
And the crows
come by with dandy
for me to make a final braid.

Erelah Emerson

Dirty Water, Poison Rain.

The distance captured my gaze as I whipped
down the highway at ninety miles per hour.
My car was barren of any sign of life.
There were no iced coffee cups or CDs.
My lighter and Marb 100s were gone.
The ashtray was pulled out, but empty.

Hundreds of miles later, the urge
to stop overcame me the way ocean
waves reclaim sandcastles along the shore.
It started in my stomach, riddling
me with fiery nausea that spread
into my throat, closing it up.
I parked my car and called it home.

I started to drink the dirty water.
I showered in it and brushed my teeth with it.
When the clouds grew heavy, I sat outside
and let the poison rain burn my skin.
The psychoactive air burned my lungs,
rewiring them to nourish my blood
with its unfamiliar chemical compounds.
At night, I let innocence be driven
out of my body like it did not belong there.

I noticed my skin cracking and peeling.
A glimmering clear, liquid seeped out of
the cracks like tears that were held in too long.
When it soaked my clothes, I ran for my car.

I ripped through branches, jumped over rocks
and tripped over roots, with my keys in my hand.

I saw my weathered down charcoal gray car
parked in the breakdown lane on the highway.
The door creaked when I yanked it open.
I slid in, dug my keys in the ignition,
and zoomed over the grass to drive straight home.

Hundreds of miles in, I felt my skin
start to pull the smaller cracks together.
My lungs burned as they pumped oxygen
back into my bloodstream. They hated it.
They wanted the power of slowing down
my brain and making my body vibrate.

The car broke down in front of my old home.
I stepped outside, the sun illuminating
the scars on my body from the poison rain.
I walked inside the house and trailed my fingers
on the wall as I walked down the hallway.
In the kitchen, I put a glass under
the faucet until it overflowed.
It spilled when I picked it up and sipped it.
The water flushed through my body, dulling
the nausea from the dirty water I drank.

Margaret Ferreira

All for the Cherry Blossoms

She wanted to escape from her home
She needed escape from her hell
She ran off
Very far away

To see the cherry blossoms

Arriving in the Far East
Alone
Quarantine lay ahead
She wrestled her demons

In hopes to see the cherry blossoms

Her monsters,
They grew
While she waited in angst
Again back at the surface

No more promise of cherry blossoms

Once she got out of quarantine
Monsters,
Demons,
Scars,
All that remained

Cherry blossoms faded

But,
They left in their wake
New green to be touched
Beneath the pain

A world waiting in vain hopes

She pleaded with her insides
To make everything go away
It all followed her across the world
Threatening sanity

Next year there will be cherry blossoms

For now she holds her tears

Stephanie Stone

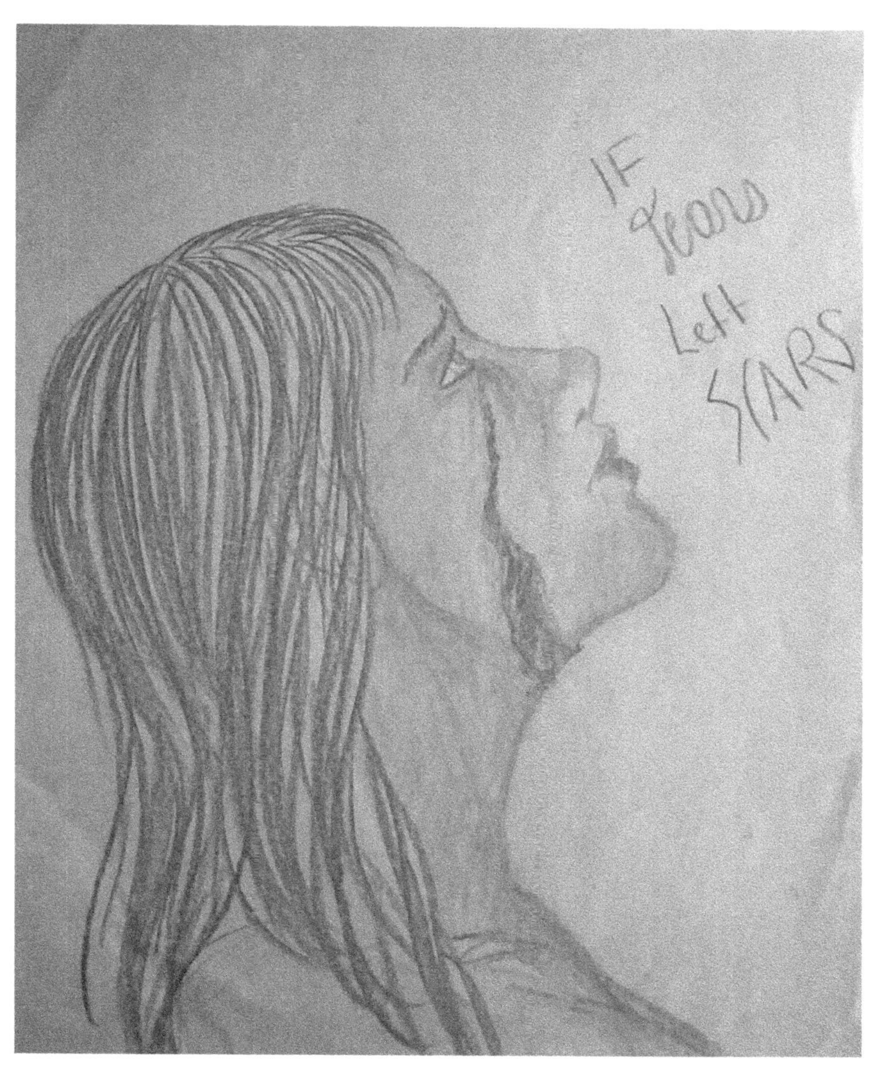

Beka Gremikova

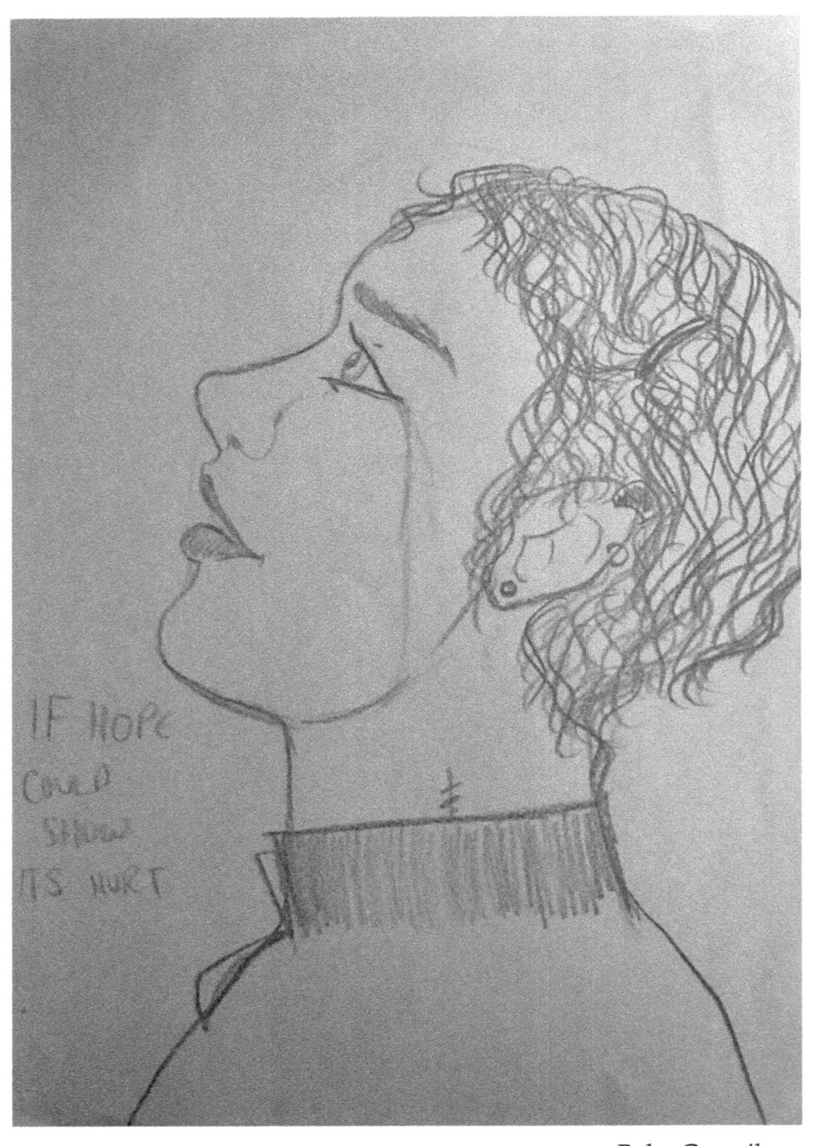

Beka Gremikova

Beach of Broken Glass

As I peer into the mirror, her words fill my mind "too fat".
As I step on the scale, her eyes see the number "too high".
And, as I drift off in the bathtub after an exhausting day at
  the gym "too lazy", she takes my hand by surprise.

I was merely floating? She convinces me I was drowning.
I can see clearly the image she's planted- myself under the
  water gasping, straining for any source of rescue.
She pulls me ashore. Offers false air to restore my lungs.
It stings as I inhale. Though it tastes refreshing- dancing on
  my tongue.
I'm no longer looking into a mirror. The flavor of something
  invigorating.

My life feels brand new.

We've met before in passing. The monster in my head and I.
  Now, she is me.
Long curly dark hair, pale skin, green sunken eyes.
I depend on her. Without me she cannot survive.
Entangled.
Like two roots growing down the same path.
Enmeshed.
Like two lovers who dare not part ways until the bittersweet
  end.
What a beautiful tragedy.
No more scale to mark my success. Now I've become
  something new.

She doesn't allow me to swim. At fear I might not return to
   the shore of "safety " she's created for us to exist on.
There's no freedom on her sand. Rules are always here.
She gives promises she cannot uphold. Screams at me with
   every change of the wind. Even the wind tries to fall silent
   in return. The wind is futile in its attempt, as I was at the
   gym.

She wants it all- my entire soul.
A beach full of broken glass has become home.
In sand of shards I play.
I pick up a handful to see blood glistening in the sun's rays.
Risking my very life. It's what she wants. And I love her.
Yet, I'd give anything to see her go. In truth, she'll never
   leave me. I must be the one to swim.
Away from the beach of broken glass.
Floating in life once again. I awake in the bathtub. Clean
   flesh, tainted soul.

Stephanie Stone

I used to swallow self love out of measuring cups,
Maintain it by a calorie limit,
And hold it a prisoner to my body by starving myself.
Now I drown myself in liberation
And remind myself that restriction and confidence do not co-
    align.
You are allowed to fall back in love with yourself and fall out
    of love with your eating disorder.

Kath Kane

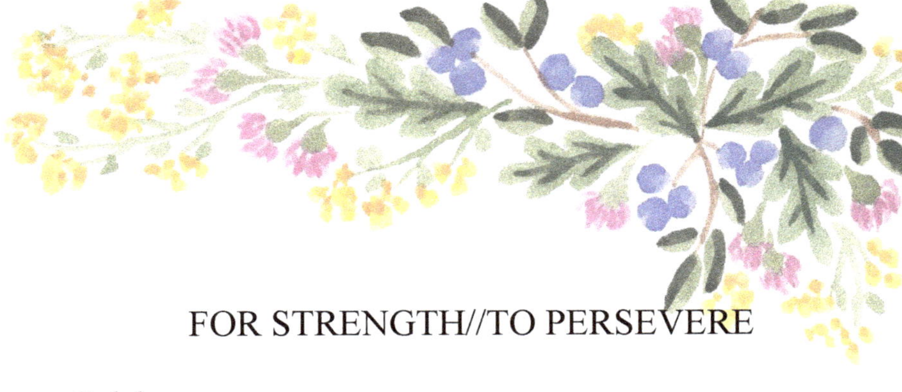

FOR STRENGTH//TO PERSEVERE

Oak leaves:

> *from humble beginnings.*
> *with patience,*
> *endurance,*
> *and strength.*

Wormwood:

> *in absence.*
> *do not be discouraged*

Thistle:

> *contrasts*
> *of pain and protection*
> *weakness and might*
> *brilliance with a rough exterior*
> *a flower and a weed.*

Blackthorn:

> *for overcoming obstacles;*
> *a better future.*
> *In the midst of devastation*
> *may there be protection and hope*

a horoscope in flowers pt. ii
blackthorn- april 19th to may 20th

you are growing taurus
gently and grounded into the earth where you were laid
it has been a difficult journey
and you are by no means at the end of it
but look how far you've come, taurus
look how strong you've gotten
your scars are still there to be remembered
but you are flourishing

Your lucky numbers are 47, 19, and 7.

From Suns to Moons

I've tried to write about this thing time and time again,
each attempt new and yellow like the delicate rays of a
dandelion.

I see fields full of us,
wanting to hold onto the floral facade long enough to be
     seen.
to be beautiful.
to be normal.
to be accepted.

If you listen, you can hear us scream "We are flowers,"
our outsides imitations.
internally, we are just weeds,
hoping our united voice will last long enough to be believed.

I've planted myself in truth,
only to discover that truth is unwelcome,
and is often plucked just before spreading.
but it keeps coming back, season after season, resilient,
persistent, until the screams fade the yellow,
and are replaced with bristles of hope.

Until the wind carries our voices and parachutes them to
     parts unknown.

to be heard,
to spread,
to take root,
and try again.

The truth;
there's nothing wrong with being a weed.

Karen Nelson

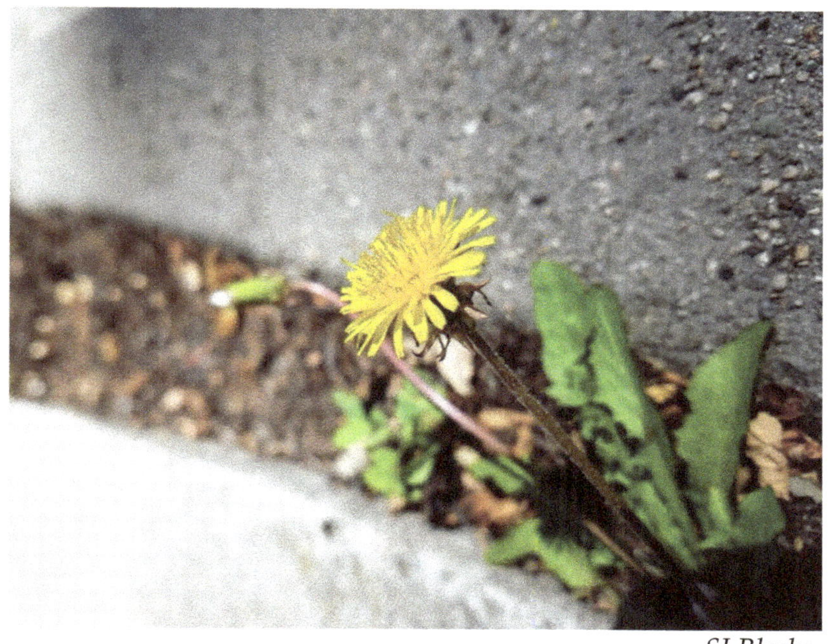

SJ Blasko

Queen Anne's Lace

When I was little I lived in a cookie cutter house that was built up so quick that it shook when the train went by. Across from it was an empty lot, beautifully overgrown, which ended in the sharp immediate plummet, twenty feet down, to the tracks below. But this edge was overgrown with blossoms, so pale and beautiful that the older kids would pick them, despite the risk of a misstep. I stayed near the road that no one drove through, with the Queen Anne's lace. It bloomed, cream colored, over the mounds, which we fancied to be hills and died in the winter with the perennial grasses. I remember a thousand dark and painful summers, and contrary to what writers and romanticisms will tell you, fear can come in summer, hate can come in summer, death can come in summer. I still think about Queen Anne's lace, even here where I never see it, I am reminded, every time I hear a train rumble past, every time I see shoes on an electric line and every time I look at the fading scars on my arms.

As they have faded, they turn to smoke, to whispers, to queen Anne's lace. I am afraid to forget how they once bloomed, afraid that I will no longer deserve help. They sit there as proof that I have hurt. No one thinks to water summer's flowers once the winter comes.

Frey Pokorny

"her words are whispers"

She whispers antagonistic words.
They trickle out like water dripping off sea salted hair
kissed by the waves at dawn.
My feet become wet.

Not everyone can hear her. To those who listen, she is
    captivating.
Every ear which can hear her does not listen equally.
To some her words are nonsense. Others hear great truth.
Until they are waist deep in rough waters. I am the latter;
    utterly stunned.

She opens her mouth, letting her whip of a tongue lash out as
    she whispers, "you're not enough."
I am enchanted.
Letting that whisper carve my soul
like a shoreline of deteriorating sand.

The volume of her whisper is deafening. Not easily ignored; I
    hear nothing else.
As her whispers ebb and flow into my system.
Outward streams the tears I bleed.
They are added to the rushing water, now up to my neck;
    strangling me like a hungry snake.

The whispers are constant. All consuming. She does not even
    pause for air.
The snake has swallowed: I am submerged now.

Her whispers are commands, "get off your lazy ass."
My mind and body are her playground. There are laws that
     only she gets to enact. Her words are whispers.
To those who listen a warning:

You will surely drown.

Stephanie Stone

Birthdays

Warmth from the candles brush my cheeks.
I scrunch my nose when the singing
becomes a competition of who
can be the most obnoxious singer

The candles weep on the white frosting.
I blow out the candles in the shape
of the numbers one and nine
unsure of where my breath came from.

The cake looks up at me in shock.
I nod, acknowledging the dysphoric,
Confused feeling in my chest that spreads up
my shoulders, my throat, and my temples
like ripples after a stone hits water.
Nineteen, nineteen, nineteen,
replays in my head like a mistake.

I expected my next milestone
to smell like flowers and chemicals,
and to taste like shitty mints, not cake.
I expected my eyes to be glued shut
and for organs to drone instead of my
family's voices singing Happy Birthday

Margaret Ferreira

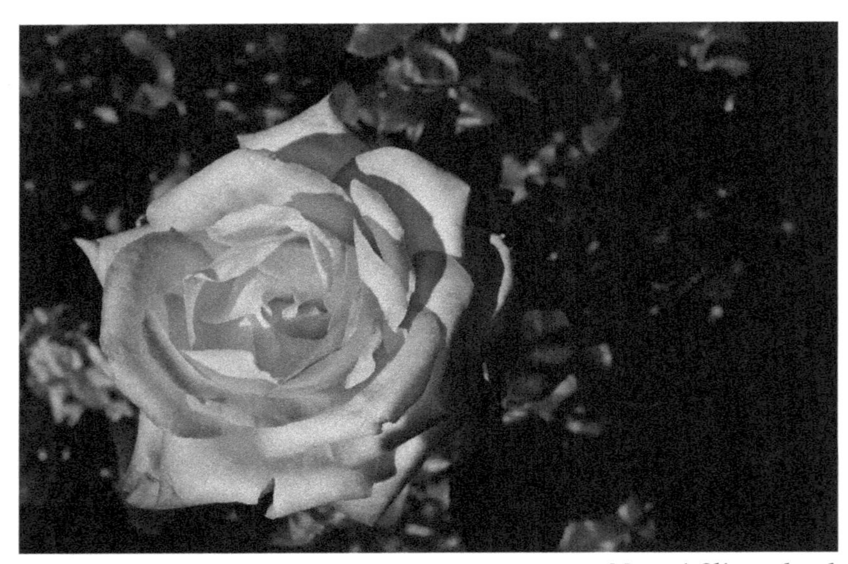

Naomi Slingerland

Shrieking Shadows

The cave was endless. No matter how many times Cara entered its darkness, the path to the surface was always a mystery, the trails too numerous and winding to remember. One rabbit trail too many, and she'd ended up here, far away from the light.

She shivered, wrapping her arms over her chest. No matter how far she ran, the chill never left the air, and sweat never streaked her skin.

But she had to keep running. Otherwise, she would lie down and succumb to the numbness.

The torches along the walls sputtered. Her stomach clenched. She couldn't face the darkness. Not alone, not again—

The torchlight vanished, plunging her into thick, cold blackness. Screaming, she grasped for a wall and leaned against the stone.

It was just darkness, she told herself. Nothing she wasn't used to. Nothing she couldn't handle.

The air froze around her, and the shadows darkened even more, sucking any remaining light from the cave. She struggled to breathe. It was *her*—

But then a voice intruded, soft and warm and familiar. *Caramia, I'm here.*

"Mamá?" She whipped her head around, searching for Mamá's salt-and-pepper hair and honey-brown skin. "Mamá, where are you?"

She's not here. A cruel voice echoed in the damp underground. *It's just you.*

Cara squeezed her eyes shut, preferring the view of the back of her eyelids to the faceless shadow before her. "Let me out."

Have you forgotten what the world is like? said the shadow. Then more voices joined, the words amplified in the darkness of her mind:

Looks like you've gained some weight, Cara. Natalie's smug words filled the air. *Eating away your problems?*

The laughter of former friends, girls who refused to associate with a loser, bounced off the cave walls.

She ran through the shadow. Its icy presence doused her in melancholy. Whimpering, she forced herself on through the passage, needing to escape the voices—

Can you just stop talking for once in your life? Tim's harsh tenor followed her, piercing to her soul. A sob hiccupped in her throat, and she bit her lip hard to keep it in. *I'm sick of it, Cara. Sick of you always talking about yourself, always asking me if I still like you. It's like you're strangling me.*

Her combat boots pounded against the slick stone, hammering with the rhythm of her heart. Tears would have blinded her if the path weren't so dark.

But each turn she took, the darkness thickened, swallowing her cries. The faceless shadow followed, brushing frigid fingers against her skin, tightening around her throat.

The refuge of her mind had become her prison.

Her own voice reverberated through the air, soft and hesitant. *Hey, Rosa.*

Her sister's silence hit Cara now, slowing her footsteps. The cave seemed to press in around her.

Um, I was wondering if you wanted to hang out, she heard past Cara say. *Play a game or something, I don't know.*

Rosalita's thick, choking silence bruised Cara's fragile heart and sliced deeper than any cruel words ever could.

Cara sank to the rocky ground. Her breaths were ragged, and her limbs were numb, weary, like she could fall asleep and never wake up. Then there would be no more pain.

You are worthless. The shadow loomed over her. *A waste of space.*

Her nails bit into her palms as she pressed her cheek against stone. Shivers wracked her body.

No one hears you. No matter how loud you scream, they won't listen. You are invisible, unnoticed, unwanted.

Cara pressed her hands to her ears, but the voices boomed around the cave, penetrating her feeble defenses. Memories, truths, all like knives digging scars into her skin.

No one would notice if you were gone.

She curled up in a ball, hugging her knees to her chest, the sounds pressing in on her like a noose. *You are nothing... nothing... nothing...*

Something brushed her cheek. She opened her eyes to find a crocus, barely visible in the dimness.

No flower should grow here—not in lightless stone. But there it was, its lilac petals straining toward her hand. Its sweet vanilla scent filled her nostrils, and she inhaled deeply, drawing strength from that whiff.

She sat up, tear-stained and shaking, and brushed its velvety petals. "How are you alive?" she whispered. "All the world is against you."

The crocus seemed to nuzzle her fingers. Biting her lip, Cara gazed at this miracle that had bloomed in the darkest and harshest of places.

The shadow loomed over her, sucking the warmth from her skin. She cupped a hand over the crocus even as the shadow strained toward it.

Give me that flower, the shadow said.

"No."

It does not belong here.

But still it lived. Still it bloomed in the shadows. And so would she.

"I do not belong here," she said, the words sudden and strange and true, echoing from a deep part of herself.

The shadow gripped her throat with icy fingers. She gasped. *You are mine,* it said. *And you will die here, alone, unwanted, unloved.*

"No!" Cara pushed through the freezing shadow and emerged on the other side, alive and warm and suddenly hungry.

The fog that had settled over her mind was lifting; she could feel herself curled up on her bed, hiding under the covers, but now light was cutting through the choking darkness. Strength and purpose began returning to her limbs. Her stomach gurgled—more hunger than she'd experienced in days.

You are weak, the shadow said. *Too weak to break free. You cannot escape me.*

A glimmer pierced the darkness. Cara ran toward it, chasing the light. From the glowing window came Mamá's tenor, gentle and warm—*I love you, Caramia. Please keep fighting.*

She would fight—like the crocus blooming in the rocky dark, she would not give up. She would fight the darkness and live.

No one cares about you, her inner voice said, a little desperately.

Come home, Caramia.

She stepped into the light.

Cassandra Hamm

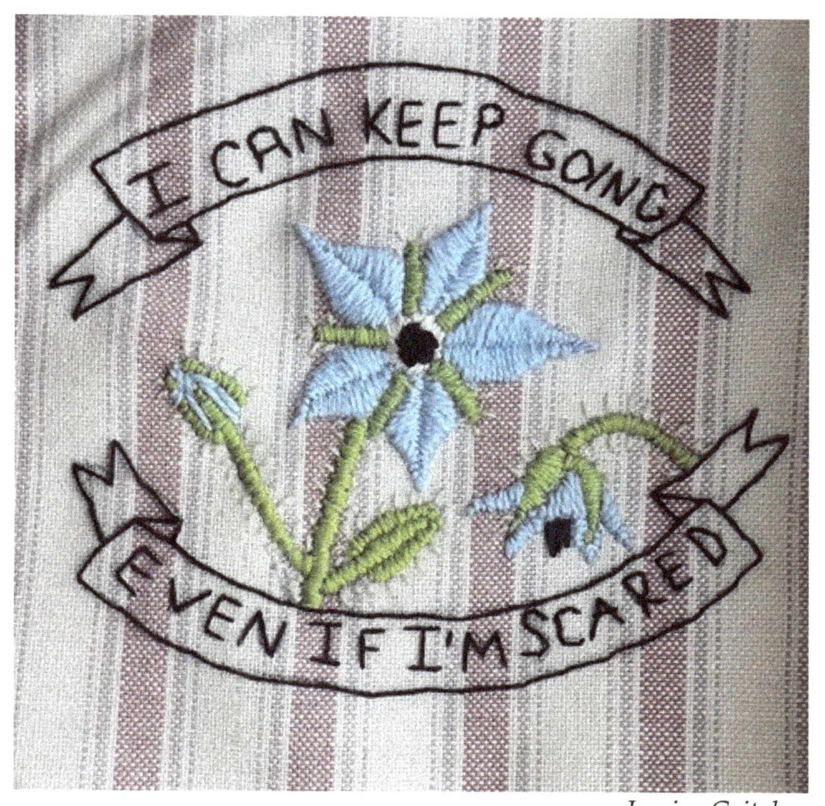

Jessica Critcher

(Medication)

If I could forget who I am,
I would do so in a second-
I want to get confused by the obstacles I see in my reflection,

I wonder how many silent kids
There are,
Promising to die-
For a God that doesn't love them,
For an answer they can't find;

Do I, too, deserve slaughter?
I know not what I mean,
But the shards are in their pieces,
And sometimes I cannot see;

I wonder then, how many have the guts to go through with
    the threat,
And I wonder if he greets them,
I wonder what they get,

Sometimes I cannot see the future;
Sometimes there's only black,
I'm starting to believe it's better
If I turned my back;

Please, someone, please tell me what I'll be greeted with at
    the lawn,
At this point
I see only laughs

And celebrations
When I'm gone;

Please tell me I'll get the chance
To disappear one day,
I'm sure things would be better
For the world, if I went away,

This war is such a quiet one,
The promises I gave,
Is a stain within the vertebrae
I tie with pink and grey,

I'll shove blackthorn down my throat,
I read,
It's supposed to cure the sick,
(To all the *thems* I know I'm failing,
I'm so sorry I exist,)

If I could forget who I am,
I'd do so before I drop,
Sometimes I forget what I'm fighting for
(but I hope that doesn't mean I should stop.)

Erelah Emerson

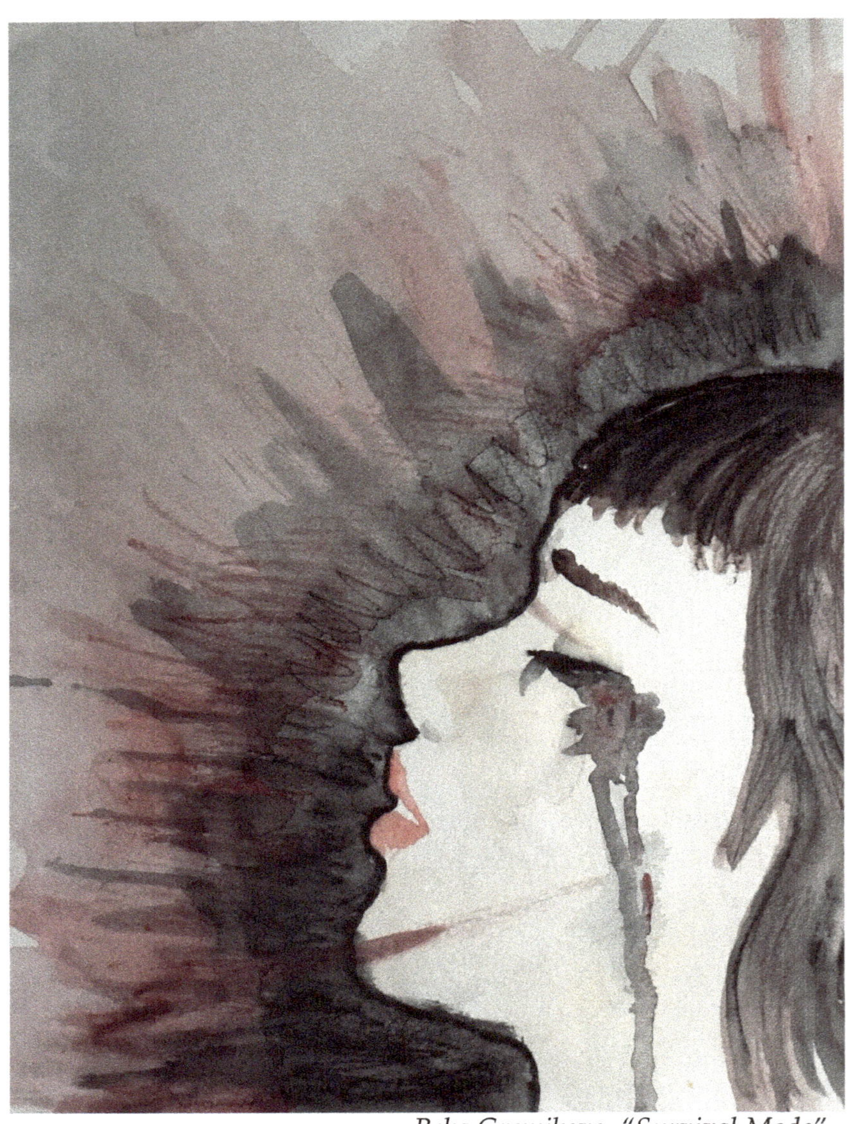

Beka Gremikova, "Survival Mode"

The Sunflower Cycle

i.

i had a dream last night
i was standing in a field bordered by wheat
the field itself, though, was full of black, loamy soil
and a woman, almost as dark as the soil she worked in
i asked her
where am i? what is this place?
and she told me
it's what you make of it. it's yours after all.
and when she went back to working
i saw a man standing in the wheat
looking at me with disdain
and so i went over to him
and i asked him
this tall, pale, sickly man who looked like death warmed
    over,
why do you frown so? what troubles you?
and he told me
she's wrong, you know it's not your field. it's a wheat field, and it
    was meant for wheat.
if you grow anything else there, it's wrong.
and so i went back to the woman, with her basket of seeds
and i told her

that man said i had to plant wheat here
and she smiled softly and said
you plant what you need to plant. but i have a feeling
that wheat will strangle your field.
and i looked at my ankles and i saw
that the bone-skinny man's wheat was tangled around them
and the woman said
it's your choice what you plant here- wheat or sunflowers
but you're gonna have to choose soon because harvest time is
     coming
wheat or sunflowers, son?
and when i started to speak, i felt the earth pulling me in
and a stalk began to grow out of the top of my head
(i woke up before i could see what it was.)

ii.
i had another dream last night
i was buried in the earth
or
maybe. not buried, but planted in the dark soil
i was not scared of being in the soil, but rather
scared of what i would grow into
the soil was warm and safe and nurturing
but i remembered what the woman said
harvest time is coming
i had to choose

whether to become a sunflower or a wheat field

and i remembered what the man said

it was meant for wheat. it's not your field

and the sunflower in me shriveled a little in my chest

and the wheat rattled around my ankles

and my heart ached

because i knew what i wanted

fields of sunflowers as far as the eye could see

but i was afraid

of what the old sickly man would say

when he saw those golden yellow petals blooming out of the
    field

i was scared of how he would act

when he saw my crown of sunlight

would he shun me? scowl at me? deny me?

would he pretend i'd planted wheat, like he told me i had to?

would my sunflowers be worth that pain?

and i heard the woman saying

it's time to wake up

harvest time is here,

and what kind of crop have you chosen, my son?

and my eyes opened up under that soil

and i looked her in the eyes

and i said,

i choose sunflowers.

iii.

i had a third dream last night

i was tending my sunflowers

pruning them, watering them, weeding them

and in the distance stood the pale and sickly man

and with a dry, hacking cough, he told me

you know, wheat wouldn't take so much effort. your sunflowers

take so much time, and wouldn't it be nice to take a break?

and i told him,

my sunflowers take time, yes

but so do all crops- my sunflowers are not special in that aspect

sometimes i see sadness in his eyes

and it makes me want to tear out every sunflower

and plant in his wheat

even though my ankles still itch from where it held me

from where, in my darkest nights with no moon to guide me,

   it creeps back

but i think of all the work i've done

planting my sunflowers, nurturing them

all the people who have told me

i have found joy in your sunflowers

and all the people they will bring joy to in the future

and perhaps one day

i will see the pale and sickly old man

smiling at my sunflowers

and on that day

i hope that i can tell him, without reservation,

i am glad that you like my sunflowers
would you like to see them up close?
and i hope that the old man can find the bravery
or if he can't, borrow some of mine
and say
yes, i would like that very much
but until then
i will take care of my sunflowers, and make them beautiful
for myself, if no one else

iv.
it has been many months since i dreamed
about the old man in my garden
but the other night he came to my sunflower fields
and he started to board them up
he had put in a fence around his own wheat
so that he did not have to see my beautiful yellow petals
and i cried *enough!*
you have desecrated my garden!
leave, and do not come back!
i chased him out of my fields
and he trampled some sunflowers as he fled
but when he left my fields seemed brighter
as though banishing him brought sunlight to my fields
maybe one day he will come back
not with a hammer and boards

but with open hands and an open heart
until then, though
i will welcome the sunlight
and the rain that will come afterwards
i will welcome my new neighbors
who harvest lilacs and violets
my war is over
and i have found some peace
(hallelujah, praise be)

Adrien Farinas

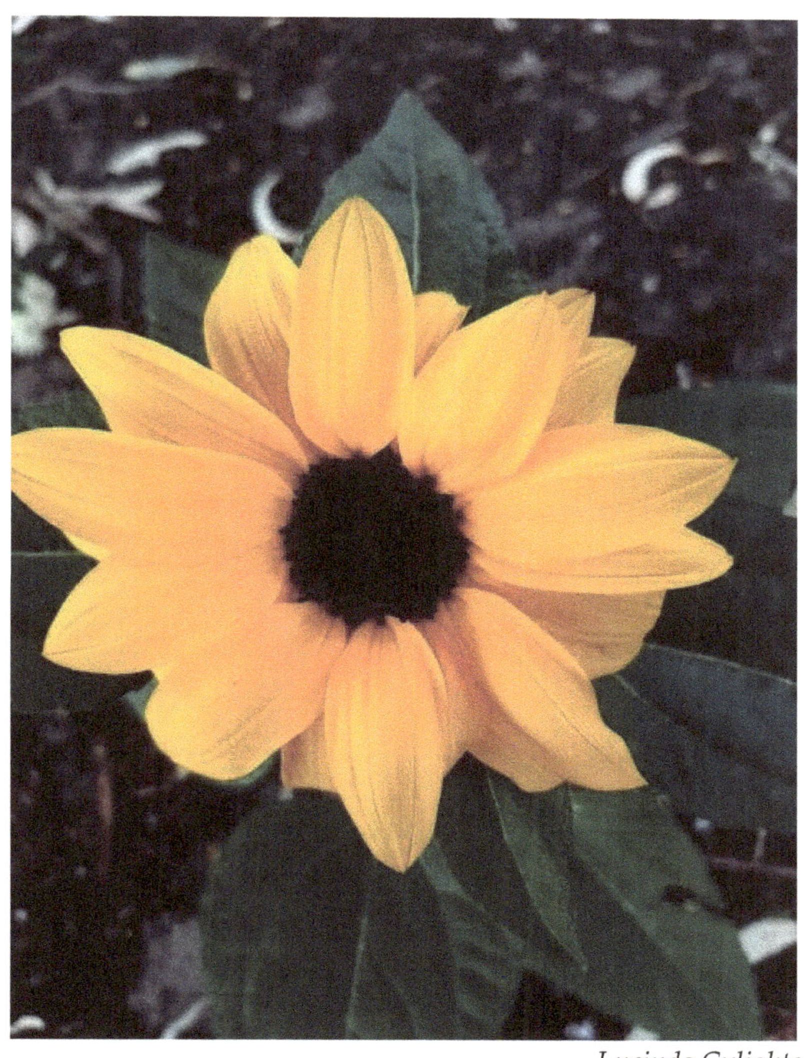

Lucinda Cylights

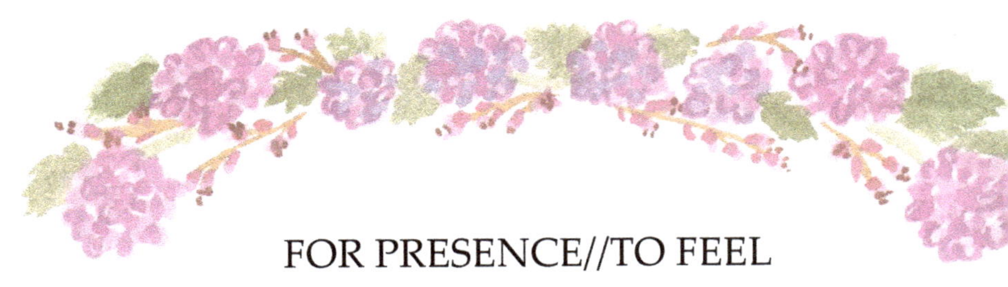

FOR PRESENCE//TO FEEL

Purple hydrangea:

the desire to deeply understand

Pink hydrangea:

with heartfelt emotion

Hydrangeas (other colors):

and gratitude

Cherry blossoms:

spring,
renewal,
and the fleeting nature of life

a horoscope in flowers pt. iii
celandine- may 20th to june 20th

oh gemini
you've really been through it haven't you
but don't be afraid
what you have been through is no small thing
in your head or outside of it
but i promise you
that in the morning everything will be at least a little better
joy comes creeping slowly in
and one day this will be a distant memory
its burden lightened with the reality you will live in

Your lucky numbers are 17, 38, and 63.

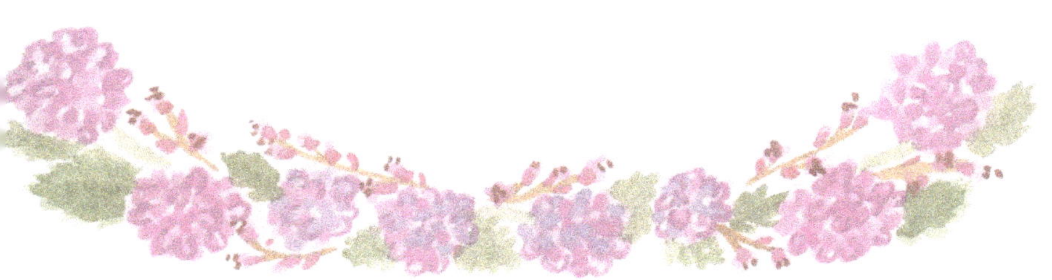

Lotus

If in the afternoon I come upon a land
and find the lotus blooming there,
Will I recognize its flowers and fruits,
I wonder.
Will I remember its story,
I wonder.
And in the evening,
after sniffing the fragrance
of the flowers and tasting the fruit,
will I have forgotten
to wonder.

Lynn White

You Are So Brave For Being Neurodiverse In My Presence

when god or the universe or whatever was handing out
brains
i didn't ask for an autistic one
jury's still out on whether i would choose this
(21 years is an awful long time to deliberate but the decision
is Important)
no one hates autistic kids! they just hate
weird   kids
they just hate kids that   won't   shut   up
about greek mythology or writing or or or
(the presence of restricted, repetitive patterns of behavior,
interests, or activities)
no one *hates* autistic kids
they just
hate *different* kids
to the point where we are considered a Terrible Trial to our
Poor Martyr Parents
A Vexation Upon This Land Brought By Vaccines
(thank you, mr. andrew wakefield. your inaccurate data lives
on to bite me back.)
i survived through fire
but not from my autism
it was from how those around me perceived it
the protea blooms in fires
but most flowers do not have this trait
meaning
the protea evolved to survive its environment
harsh and cruel and brutal

perhaps in a kinder world
we would see its beauty without its pain
(perhaps in a kinder world we would not have to be savants
to receive human dignity)

Adrien Farinas

Fire

The   pair   of   eyes   beget
The   pair   of   rocks
The   friction   of   which
Brings   forth
The   primeval   fire   indeed

A   matter   of   regret   is   that
At   the   very   outset
Fire   burns   itself

A   matter   of   solace   is   that
As   in   the   case   of   fire
That   being   fact
The   ashes   keep   no   regret.

Guna Moran

Translated by Bipul Kumar Baruah

Mercy of the Forest

i am a broken mirror
of glass shards scattered on the floor
squeaky wooden boards & unhinged oak doors
think not to understand me
i barely comprehend myself
instead listen to my muddy footsteps
as they practice the art of stealth
you will find me in abandoned mansions
with ivory pillars coated in vine
you will find me in dense forests
covered in deciduous trees & pine
so as your feet dangle off that bridge
'jump' i'll whisper, 'join me instead'
so you'll crash down to the ripples & the tide
feeling all the things you couldn't when you were alive
call me your conscience, your darkest tendency
i am a second chance, what would death be without mercy?

Kalandfitz

Her Marigold Form

Trapped in skin
It treats me like a leash
Trapped by my appearance
The mirror unavoidable
She walks by
Perfect
The marigold sensations bubble to the surface
I feel it all
Here, I am trapped, caught, stuck
While she galivants
In marvelous form
The marigold formed creature
Becomes a new expectation
Someone who I compare myself to
Someone who I assume has everything
Days pass
The marigold creature torments me
I'm trapped and,
Wilted
Days fade into months
And I realize
Marigolds wilt, too

Stephanie Stone

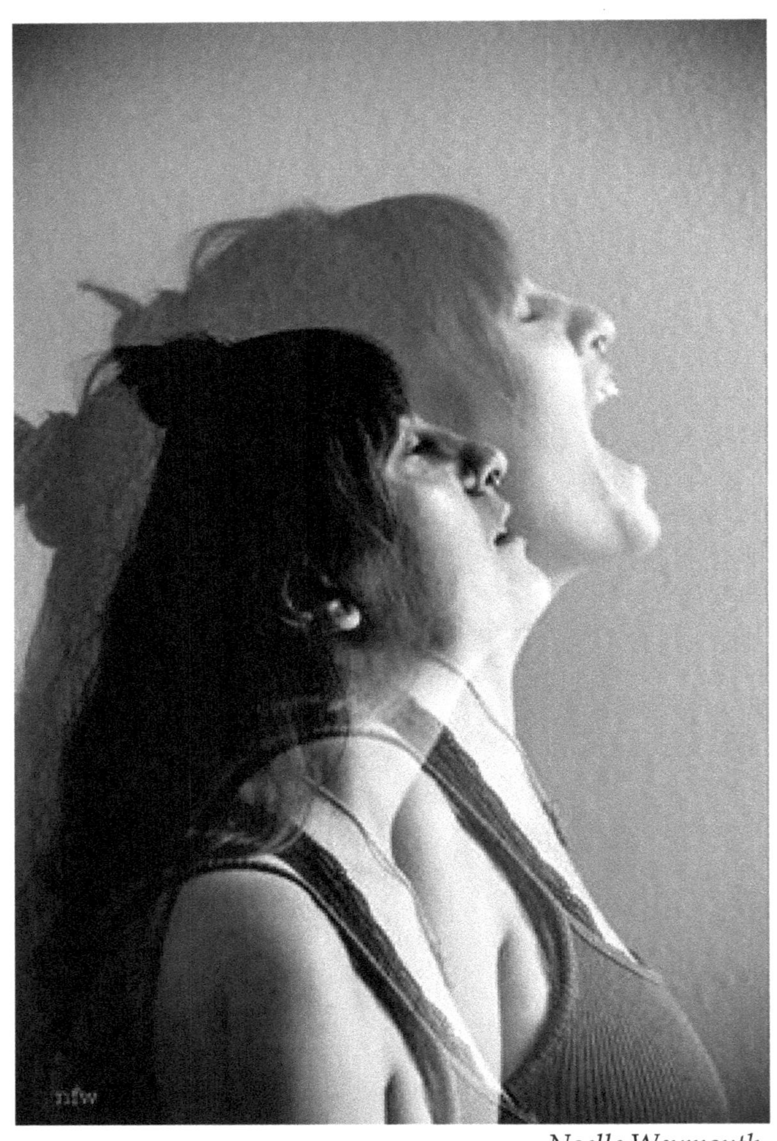

Noelle Weymouth

Savanna

I feel like a shell of a person,
A hole of what once was,
A shallow boned piece of broken love.

Noelle Weymouth

Plumeria

The morning burns
your eyes and throat
and tired starts to seep,
Yet you're still searching for the antidote
that will put you to sleep

you do not wonder
what the night looks like-
(you see it in the chime)
And the mysteries in dark hallways
became your friends with time;

You think you'll always know exactly
when the clock
will ring,
you've been counting down the seconds
since you've forgotten
how to dream.

But there will always be the nighttime,
there's no reason to be
tied to the dark,
Afraid that one day
you'll close your eyes
and you'll lose that special mark

It's not a choice to find yourself
stuck in shrouds of sleepless hours

Maybe you think
closing down your mind
might take
away your nighttime flowers-

You'll see plumeria
twist up the spine
Of trees that's crawl and creep-
And maybe soon,
playing the violin for the moon
Will be enough to help you sleep.

Erelah Emerson

flowers don't grow in an organized way

the body which i have grown / has adopted flower seeds. /
into eye sockets: / little tiny fingerfuls of violet, buttercup, /
camellia. / i imagine they will grow quietly / out of the space /
and kiss the palms / of my hands someday / nurtured by the
water / in my soft tissues / and the sunlight shining / on where
my eyes used to be / like a painting.

and yet they are never organized in such a way, / sprouting in
all different directions, / out of every orifice—there's never a
moment / where i don't ache / knowing that they just go
where they want—/ but the flowers are mine. / and when my
teeth are rose thorns, / when my kisses feel like rainwashed
petals / and my tongue is made of lavender, / when i touch my
face and feel like i am real / or look in the mirror and stop
holding my breath,

the seeds will have begun to blossom.

Angelina Luo

Search Party

Somebody is missing.
Sometimes I think I catch a glimpse of her,
that person I used to be.
She runs ahead into the light
laughing, just out of reach, begging me to follow her
out of the darkness, the room,
the bed.

Occasionally she sends a message,
a postcard, telegram,
distress signal.
I can't stop looking
because I know she can be found,
out there somewhere.

When I can I search for her
at therapy sessions, clinics, the bottom
of a wine bottle.

She has to be out there somewhere.
Perhaps she's looking for me
and I am not there to find.
I search for an emotion, a movement
a heartbeat.
Occasionally I hear something – a message, a plea.

But I stay here, in the dark, in this room,
this bed.

I don't remember how to laugh,
although I remember how it feels.
And the light hurts my eyes,
yet sometimes I think I catch a glimpse of a world I used to
    know.

Somebody is missing.

Sarah Hindmarsh

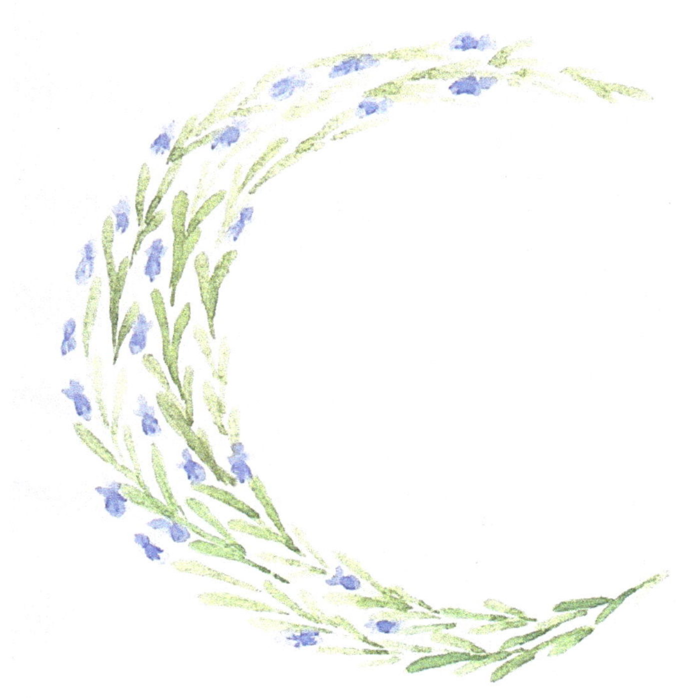

Naomi Karsudjono

While Gardening

The thorn of a rose-bush caught me this morning
while gardening
squarely in the backside, of course,
it tends to happen that way
And I arose, at once, indignant and feeling foolish
(my pride overtakes me at times, I'm sorry to say)
and as I tended to my hurt
(which was only my pride, really)
a smile arose,
and a laugh too
that bubbled up from somewhere deep, that rambling brook
of the good, strong variety
that heals and helps
and so the rose,
in all of her complex parts
reminded me, once again,
of the silliness of this life.

Theo Oliver

FOR ENDINGS//TO GRIEVE

Marigold:

> *passion and creativity,*
> *grief and mourning,*
> *sorrow and despair.*

Amaranth:

> *"one that does not wither"*
> *--from the greek, amarantos.*
>
> *also known as "love-lies-bleeding"*
> *and used to convey hopelessness*

Rosemary:

> *remembrance*

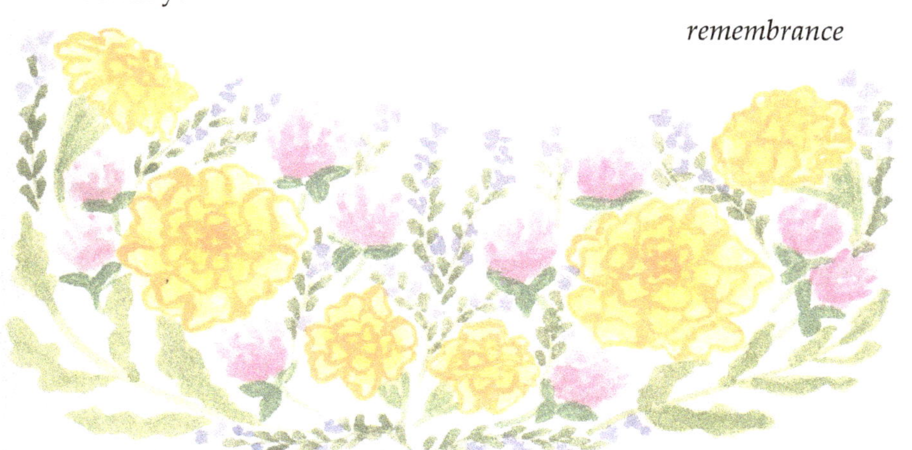

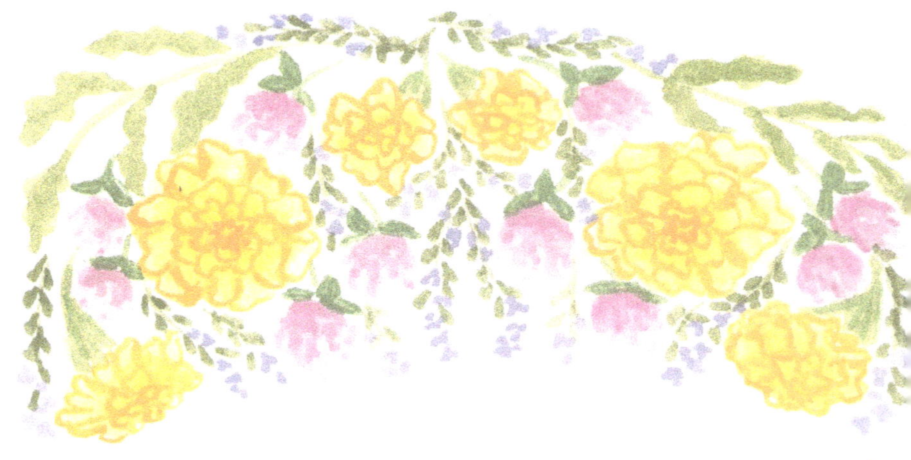

a horoscope in flowers pt. iv
pink hydrangeas- june 20th to july 22nd

you always feel so much, cancer
the emotions bowling you over with their strength like a ship
    in a storm
but the important thing to remember
is that the highs and the lows come together
the biggest triumphs do not erase the heartbreak you've
    faced
nor do the hardest tragedies scrub out
the joyful and gentle fingers of the morning
clutch them gently, cancer
as though you would a partner's hand
and keep going through this dance we call life

Your lucky numbers are 73, 54, and 9.

I used to search for the grave of all the things I used to love.
Now I look in gardens and hope that they have grown.
I hope that they have bloomed and enveloped someone else's
    time,
That their roots have broken through the surface,
And that the skeletons find a home to create themselves
    again behind closed doors.
Just because they were once loved by me doesn't mean they
    have to die.
I am working on helping others grow,
Now that I have blossomed.

Kath Kane

Remembrance

This afternoon, if I come across a pool
of still water
and find the lotus blooming there,
I will scatter rosemary
on the surface
so that I don't forget
to remember
me.

Lynn White

Get Well Soon

Joe:
i am learning to tend flowers by my mother's mouth.
    two birds share a nest inside my ceiling: mum &
daughter. their new eggs are laid in my head.
flowers twinkle like many stars doing a jazz choreography…
hallucinations.

Jane:
mum lay on the sickbay- stroked.
    by her window, in the ward. i sing her to bed. and unseen
shadows between her sleeping and waking.
doctors cock their syringes like angry rifles in the morning. i
turn away my face.

Jason:
a matchstick strikes the back of the sun-
    the candles in my head glow.
for this, hope is the wing that bears the weight of a grieved
heart.
many are the miseries haggling in the minds of people;
blurred, dimmed & suicidal.

Julian:
the light after a tunnel is the one your eyes can see: sparks of fleeing stars.

a warm hug & a cup of coffee trades love to one whose heart trembles with aloneness.

everyone deserves to point to a star that wears their name at night.

Ojo Olumide Emmanuel

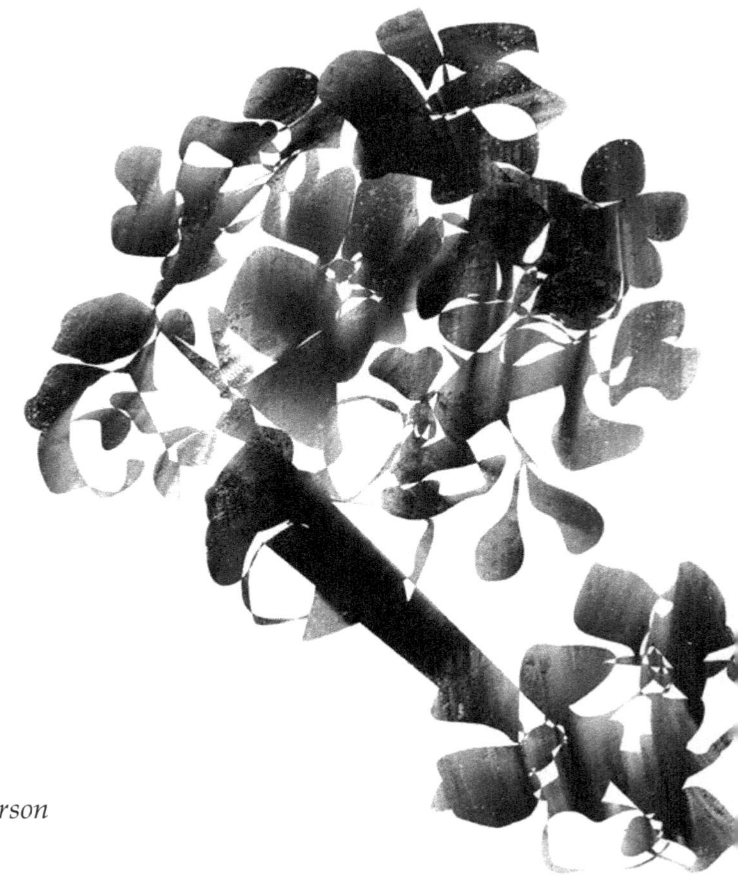

Erelah Emerson

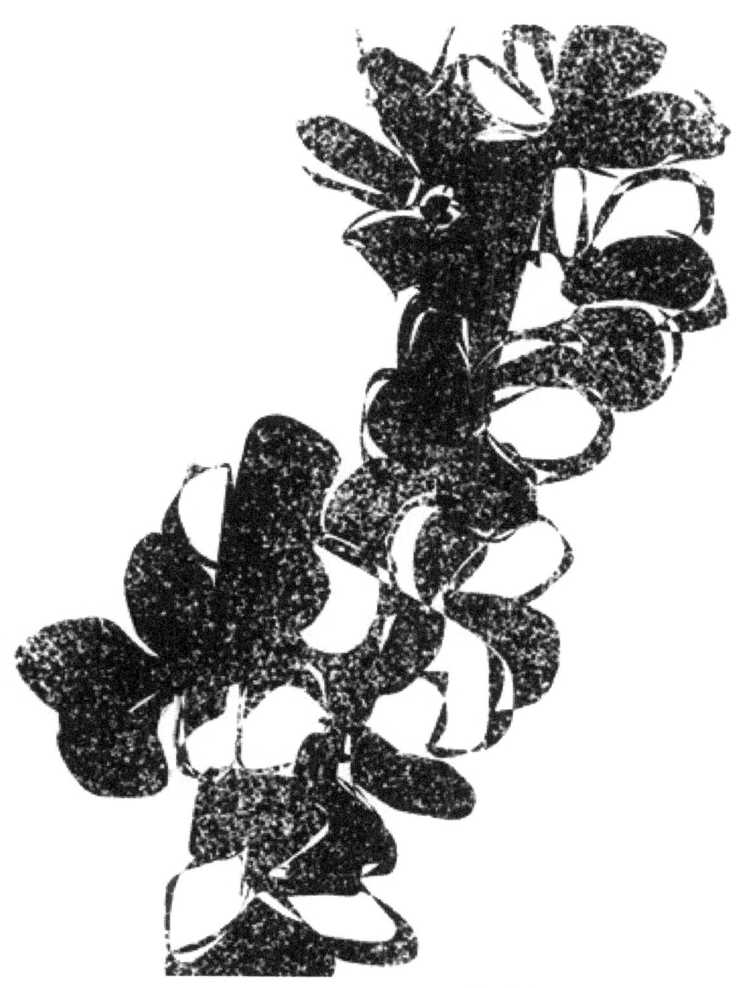

Erelah Emerson

Windflower

if I cannot save you
if I cannot save myself
I will turn my tears to flowers for you

flowers like beneath
our bare feet that one time we
decided to run away, live with wood-fairies
(tree sap and stolen seconds)

flowers like purple-petal breeze
whispering back our secrets
on the river bank
rustles and ripples
fading to echoes
and the wind traced *we will follow*
onto our palms

flowers like wilting
while i lay superglued
counting the threads in my sheets
crushing my corneas on ceiling corners

like pressed in pages;
you found them
brittle
and brown
and broken
and from that day
the pieces lived in your eyes

like crushed
beneath our feet
rat-racing to freedom
darling, we killed so many things
and we should have known
should have known

flowers—never to line paths
to our moss-mushroom cottage
flowers—I will not weave
with your curls at nightfall
flowers—I refuse
to drop in the dirt for you

instead i will
turn my tears
to dream-violet flowers
they will fly
with you
ease you
into night sky
they will drape you
a blanket, summer-light

they will rest on the ground
playground foundation
for tomorrow's anemones

my tears will not be empty
my hands will not be empty

every breath—
every heartbeat—
every dream—

i will turn them to flowers for you

Polina Litvak

Grief

Break, bend,
even shout, if you must,
and, when you have finished your heart's work of grief, go
    out to the garden,
where the blue jay has just landed, just now, in the grass…
and is singing.

Theo Oliver

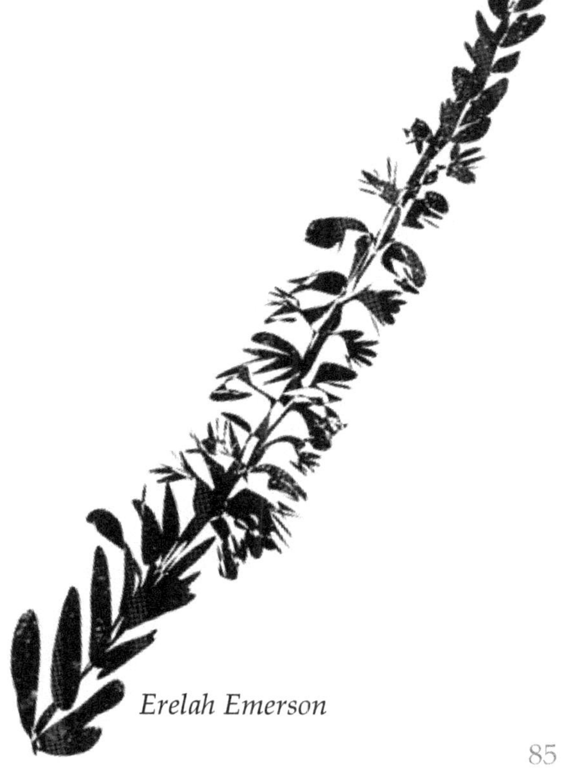

Erelah Emerson

Always Barefoot Across the Fields of Thistles

Here. This is the place.
Leave your shoes with me.
The field is thick with prickles
and it is getting dark.
You must walk down all the way
and then walk all the way back.
You might wonder if I will be
here waiting for you
Well take comfort in knowing
that I will not.
You will go anyway, alone,
all the way down and all the
way back, barefoot across
my field of thistles.
You ask if you could take
the road. This is the road, I say.
The thistles are the only way.
And you know that even today.

Tiberius

Ark

A shell
A wall
An empty threat

You were my hands
You were my voice

Never shunning
Never discerning
Never a question until there was

But a foundation can still be stood upon
Even after being shaken

Come now
There's work to be done

R. Sunshine

"Oh, you're THAT Suzy!"

Sometimes, when I can't sleep, my brain decides it's the perfect time to lace up its walking shoes and take a stroll down memory lane. (After all, isn't 2:00 a.m. the perfect time to relive that awkward moment from 7th grade?) I find myself sorting through memories I didn't realize I'd held onto. As each memory bubbles to the surface, I let myself imagine what would have happened if things had turned out differently.

For a while, I've been wondering how to tell this story; wondering if I should tell this story at all. It's one of those cringe-worthy moments that's been keeping me awake at night. I am still processing it but I'm going to share it anyway. In the end, I think, maybe, it says something about the power of shame and the importance of forgiveness.

A few weeks ago, I got a friend request on Facebook from a guy I knew in college. After accepting the request, I noticed that we had a few friends in common. Much to my surprise, there on his list, was a very significant ex-boyfriend. After a few online chats, I asked him about my ex. He explained their connection and then asked how I knew him. I told him we'd lived together for a few years. We had even been engaged. As a point of reference, I said, "We lived together in the little brick duplex." He was quiet for what felt like a very long time and then a single sentence appeared on my screen. It simply read, "Ooooh, you're THAT Suzy!"

I was caught off guard and couldn't process what he'd said quickly enough to respond. The rest of the conversation is a blur. Afterward, I rolled his words around in my head - THAT Suzy – and the shame settled over me like fog. I knew that he hadn't meant to be unkind, but his casual description spoke volumes about my history. He was describing much of my life before I received a proper mental health diagnosis.

Sadly, I understood exactly what he meant. The memories of that time came flooding back. I remember going days without sleep, being paranoid and confused. I also remember going weeks without being able to get out of bed, unable to shower or brush my teeth. I have a very odd but specific memory of crying inconsolably for a solid week after watching a documentary about snow monkeys; how something about the human-like appearance of their hands had made me feel sad and fragile. I remember so many crazy things I said and did; all the times I embarrassed him in front of his friends and family. I also remember waking up to find a tube down my throat, pumping my stomach after an overdose. I remember listening to the doctor explain that I'd be held for 72 hours in the psych ward of our local hospital. Over the doctor's shoulder, I can still remember my boyfriend's face: tired, sad, frustrated, and frightened. I'm sure he had experienced the onset of my illness quite differently than I had. Even though I will always remember those years as some of the most painful of my life, I had to admit to myself that "THAT Suzy" probably did sum up his memory of me.

For the first time, I allowed myself to really examine those years. I spent quite a few sleepless nights reliving, with red hot shame, so many things I'd said and done. Then, quite unexpectedly, I recalled a bit of advice someone gave me, a long time ago: treat yourself with the same kindness you'd treat someone else - someone you love.

Treat yourself with the same kindness you'd treat someone else.

That's not as easy as it sounds. We are often our own worst critics. There are times when we can be very cruel to ourselves. Still, in the nights that followed, I tried to view my story from a distance. What if that girl wasn't me? How would I judge her actions?

Late at night, I let her story unfold. I watched this troubled girl trying desperately to find her footing. I listened to her search for the language to describe what was happening to her. I began to realize that she wasn't just someone's crazy ex-girlfriend. She was a young woman who didn't understand what was happening to her. She needed help. It really was that simple.

It wouldn't be true to say that I don't still feel a bit uncomfortable when I think about some parts of my past. Some memories will always be painful to revisit. Even so, for the first time in my life, I finally have a lens through which I can view my past with compassion. I might always be THAT Suzy to some people, but that doesn't have to define me. For many, I will be THIS Suzy - a million miles from perfect but further along my path than before.

I wish I could go back and tell that lost girl that things will get better. I wish I could tell her about all the good things that are going to happen to her. I guess maybe I owe my Facebook friend a debt of gratitude. If not for his off-the-cuff remark about my time in that little brick duplex, I might never have been able to forgive that lost girl.

Suzanne Lea

I have a history
Of over-watering plants
Long dead from lack of care
Hoping hoping hoping to atone
Praying I might bring them back

But in learning to let go
To let things gone be gone
Sometimes I am too quick to cut myself
From things that still have life in them

I knew
That succulents understood what it was like
To be dry, to be silent, to be bones
To shed petals
Curl leaves
Drop tendrils, shoots and buds
And retreat
Holding that which is important all the closer

But I have underwatered mine,
As I have underwatered myself
Passing by and leaving falling leaves
on read, with no response.
A few have passed beyond the veil
And I shed my tears as I return them to the earth
But some of them surprise me
And there is a comfort in the knowledge
That something which has grown to withstand drought
Has not been killed by me.

SJ Blasko

Crocus

Maybe one day you'll be walking in a forest,
maybe one day you'll feel safe
enough to venture beyond the doors
And take,
and take,
and take,

my body won't be far behind you,
I will always be around,
even if I do not want it,
even if
I'm only sound,

And maybe, if you're lucky,
there will be no noisy scream
of an older, dying elder tree
that died for being mean

Maybe one day you'll be able
to walk along the lines
where you never thought to venture,
where you thought
you'd be a crime,

I cannot tell you what this feels like,
I cannot tell you it's okay,
maybe
you got to the forest
but I was washed away,

Maybe one day, you'll be walking,
and you won't have set in mind
that the end
is what you're walking towards
(thoughts so much like mine)

My ashes are a free for all,
when you are walking by the lake-
Please find out where the crocus grows and take
and take
and take.

Erelah Emerson

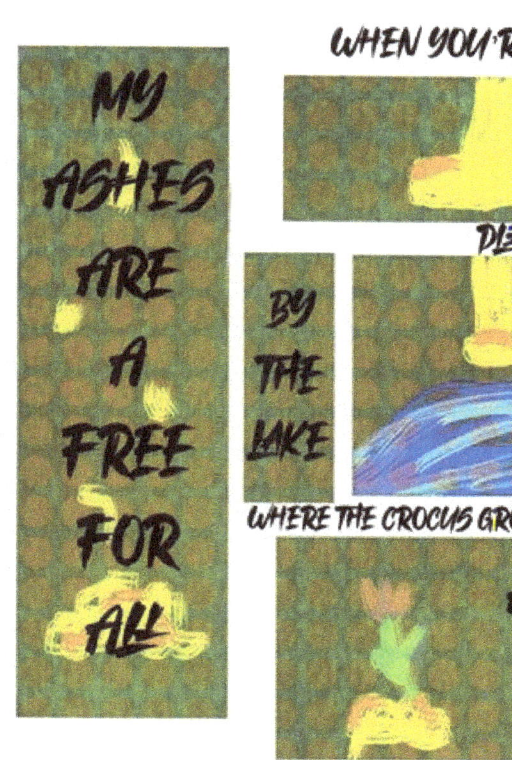
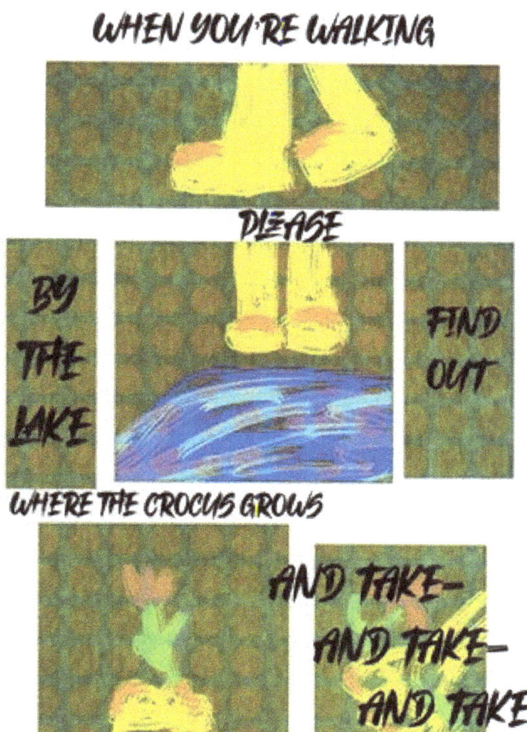

Erelah Emerson

Bouquet

The flowers from your mom's funeral still hang upside down
from the basement ceiling, dangling over the sink. You left
them there to dry so you could press them between pages,
create bookmarks out of the worst day of your life.

Then you forgot. And you continue to forget, even though
you see those flowers almost every day. It's another addition
to your to-do list, another piece of your depression that
hasn't been fixed. Of your anxiety that hasn't been lessened.

One day you'll snap. Just like how you let your room turn
into a cesspit and live there still, because you don't have the
energy or motivation to care. Until you hit a Good Day and
you feel Better and you whip through like a Tornado and
everything is clean and you can almost believe that you are
Thriving for once.

Then the fog returns. And you forget what Good Days
look like, because all you can see are dead flowers all around
you—broken relationships, unknown future. Where do you
fit, in this scattered mess of strewn petals and broken stems?

You don't know.

But.

You build small pieces of happiness for yourself.

.

You write. You draw. You plan your next trip across the world.

Because as long as you believe there are things to look forward to, that you won't be slogging through the mire forever—it's easier to push through the fog. It's easier to offer grace to yourself on the hard days.

It's easier to pick up those strewn petals and broken stems and drop them in the compost pile. It's easier to go to the store and buy yourself a beautiful bouquet.

To soak in the beauty, instead of the blame.

Beka Gremikova

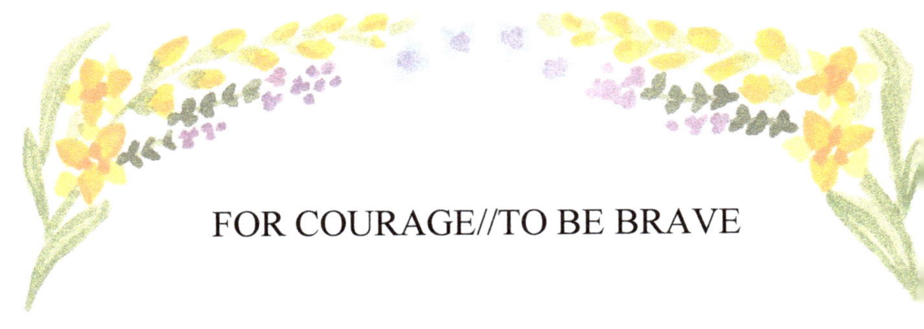

FOR COURAGE//TO BE BRAVE

Borage:

courage, peace, tranquility

Thyme:

courage
derived from the greek, thymus

Gladiolus:

strength and integrity.
associated with the qualities of gladiators

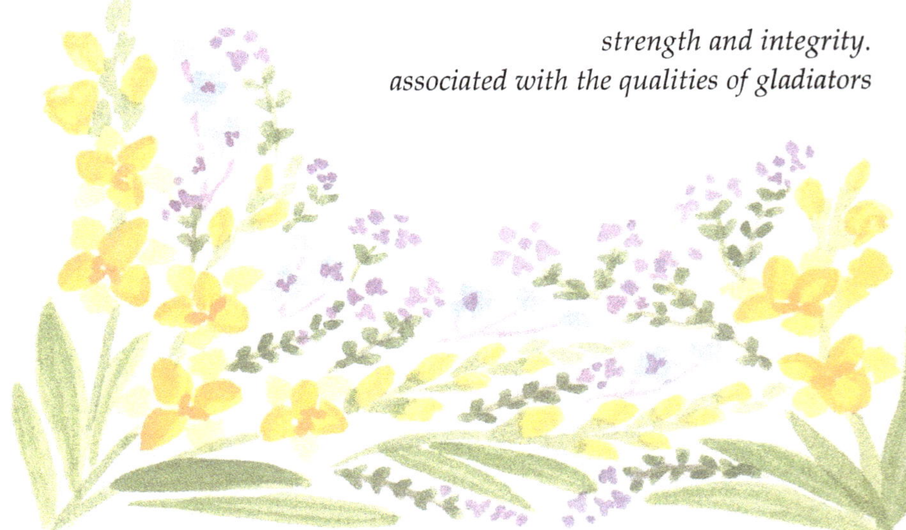

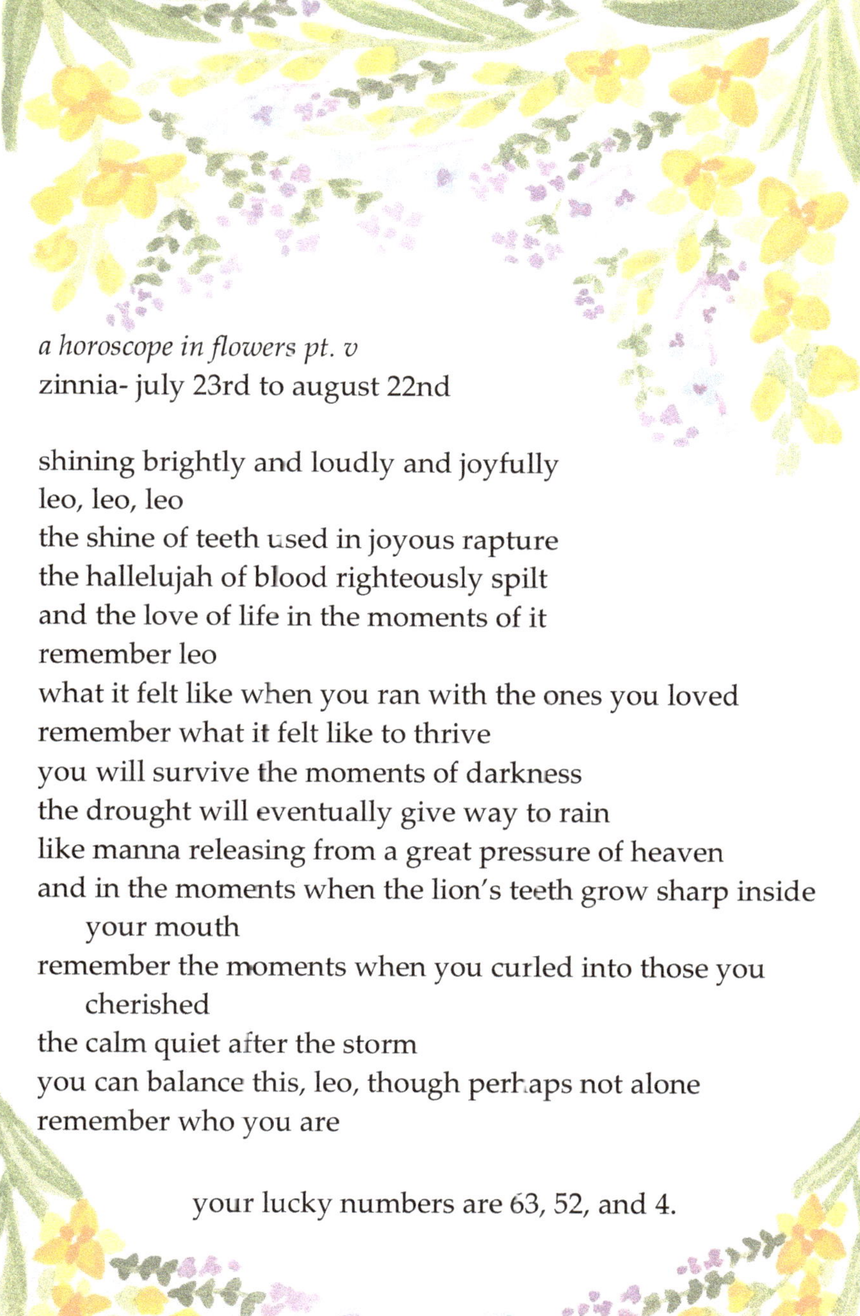

a horoscope in flowers pt. v
zinnia- july 23rd to august 22nd

shining brightly and loudly and joyfully
leo, leo, leo
the shine of teeth used in joyous rapture
the hallelujah of blood righteously spilt
and the love of life in the moments of it
remember leo
what it felt like when you ran with the ones you loved
remember what it felt like to thrive
you will survive the moments of darkness
the drought will eventually give way to rain
like manna releasing from a great pressure of heaven
and in the moments when the lion's teeth grow sharp inside
     your mouth
remember the moments when you curled into those you
     cherished
the calm quiet after the storm
you can balance this, leo, though perhaps not alone
remember who you are

          your lucky numbers are 63, 52, and 4.

Dichotomy of Queen Anne's Lace

Lovely and showy filigree
stand tall and flock together,
Wizened head bent lowly,
Emotional bellwether.

Parts unfurled and exultant,
seek sunshine and the rain.
Emotions left unpent,
Soon curled in self-disdain.

Not unlike sweet Queen Anne's Lace
I find myself in twain.
Half the time I love myself,
the rest, I fight the pain.

Maggie D Brace

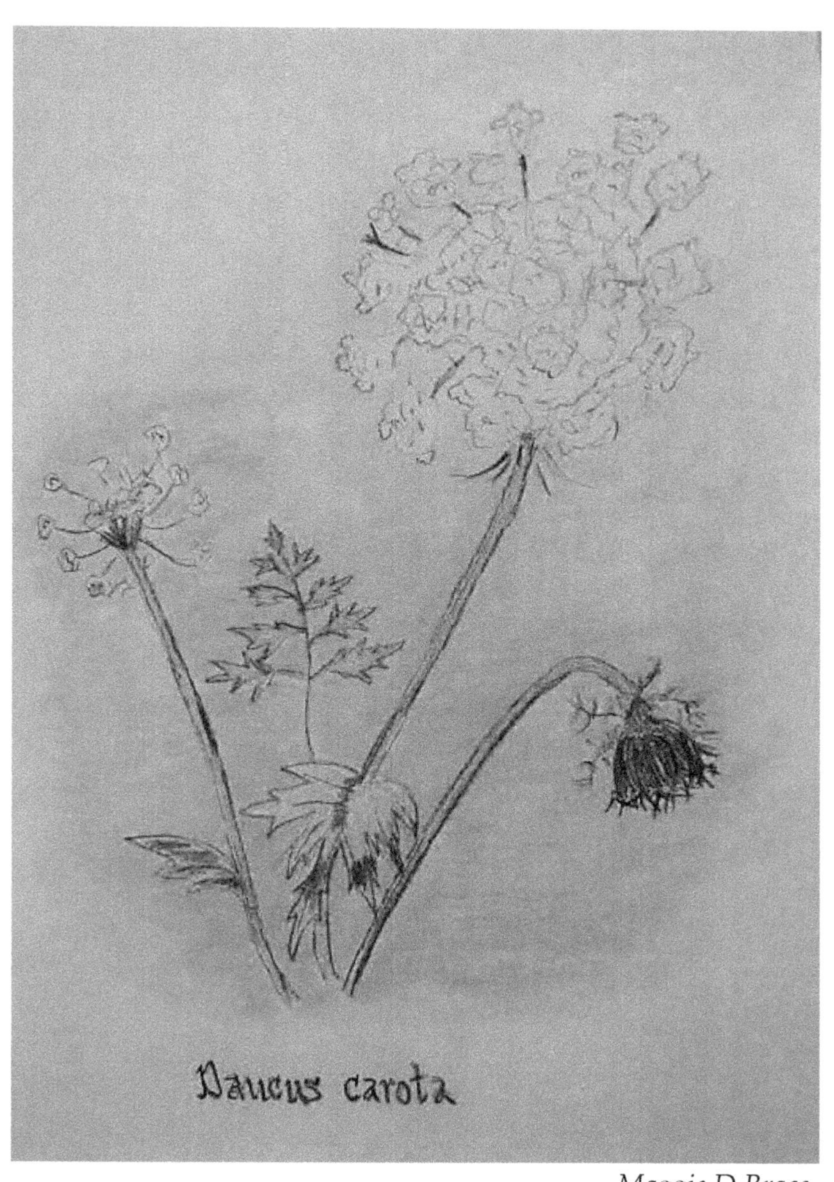

Daucus carota

Maggie D Brace

Recovery

       Reality

It all starts from the bottom; the rocky, sharp flooring. Every breath is caught by your own being, shakily holding it until it's let go. A day goes by, thousands of shaky breaths, trembling hands and silently crying to yourself. Because, *you have to do this for yourself.*

And while things start coming easier, sometimes your brain will wander back into the dark woods, falling off path. Jagged rocks are in your eyesight, your body urges you to run. But, which way? Hands tremble, though your heart stays steady. *Let's just take a seat.*

It's bright outside, the sun looks for you under the trees, peeking under leaves. Your path is clear now, your mind quiet; which also makes you uneasy. *But, this time you let it.*

The path is soft, pillow-like; the climb starts going uphill. Daisies and sunflowers bloom on either side of you, your nose flooded with sweet floral scents. You find the sound of birds being the only thing that fits in your eardrum.

Pebbles litter the path, but you see the top of the hill. It's so close, you need it, you have to get better—the calculator pops in your mind, a freeze frame from lunch. Too many items, a flavored beverage even. ~~God, what did you do?~~

Clouds form above you, thunder cracks as you slip, slipping down the hill. You grasp for pebbles, clinging for dear life. Pleas exit your mouth as if this landslide is only your words, *"I want to be better. I have to be better. I can't go back to that place."*

The clouds separate, the sunflowers reach for warmth and so do you. This hill will not destroy you. *Your past will not drag you down further than you let it. You can drag yourself out of those jagged, sharp corners. Sunshine will always come, looking for you in the darkness.*

—your resilience shields you from thorns.

Kimmy Renee

holding Buddha
on eight petals
these dark days
I ask for the strength
of a lotus

Jackie Chou

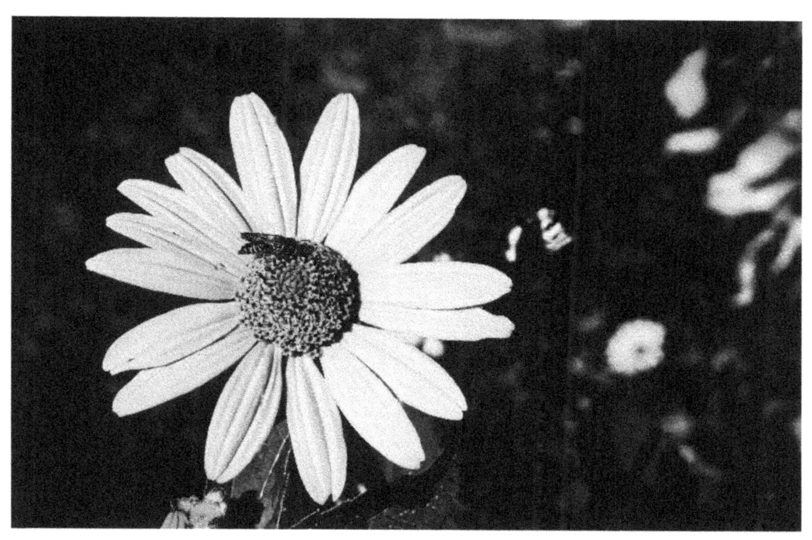

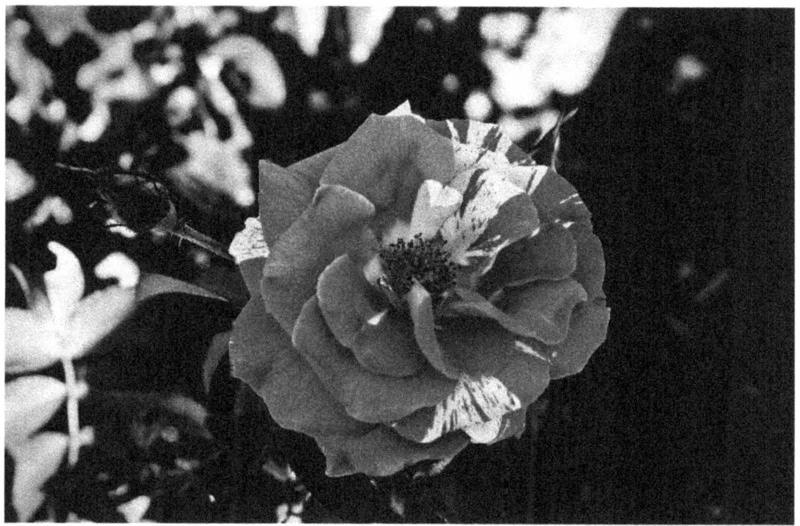

Naomi Slingerland

Walls

I am a dam
No one can reach me
For I have built
W A L L S
Around myself.
I am constantly filling
And now-
Now I am on the brink.
I am going to overflow.
But then-
Something catches my eye...
D A I S I E S
Bright.
Cheerful.
Happy.
Nothing like my dam.
My dam that is rolling with waves,
Stirred by my internal storm,
And about to overflow.
My dam-
The dam, that is, in essence, me-
Calms for a moment.
D A I S I E S.
They show me a smile
A laugh
A hug
L O V E.

"Maybe," I think.
Maybe, just maybe,
My dam doesn't have to
O V E R F L O W
And instead
I can
Let it trickle
S
L
O
W
L
Y
Out
Until
There is no dam.
No walls.
No storm.
Just me-
Me and my daises.

- Hold onto your daisies.

Lucinda Cylights

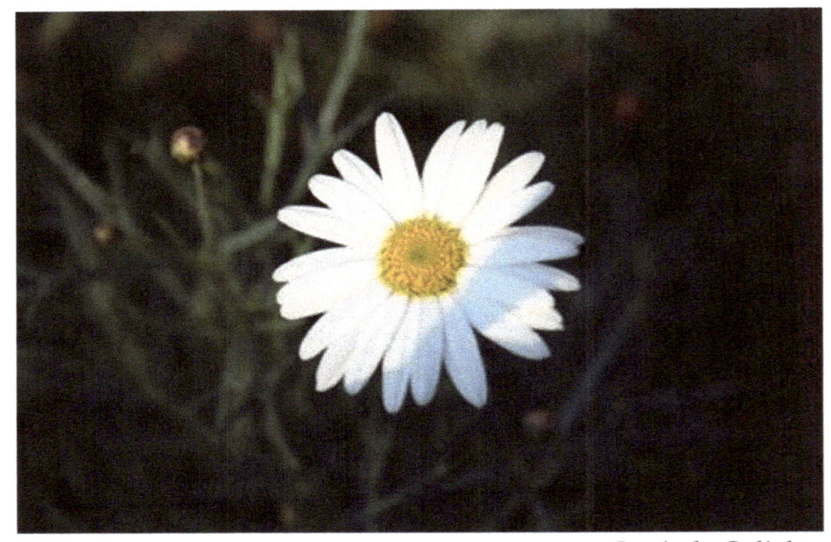

Lucinda Cylights

Toward the Sun

Sometimes on the darkest days
When sunny skies reflect the night,
I feel the tugging on my roots
And start my dreary downward flight.

To waters where the creatures lurk,
Their faces hidden by their deeds.
They fill me with their darkest thoughts
Until I rest among the reeds.

From underneath the vibrant world,
Where in decaying hands I lie,
I see the secrets that we keep
From birth until the day we die.

Beneath the hues of living flowers
Sit the haunting shades of black.
They push away all vital colour
Weighing down until we crack

I lift myself from lifeless hands
And cut the tethers from my soul
Until I rise, my bonds cut free,
To join the flowers that are whole.

Days go quickly, life moves on,
For fleeting moments I feel I've won,
And when the tugging comes once more,
I turn my face toward the sun.

Nathaniel Luscombe

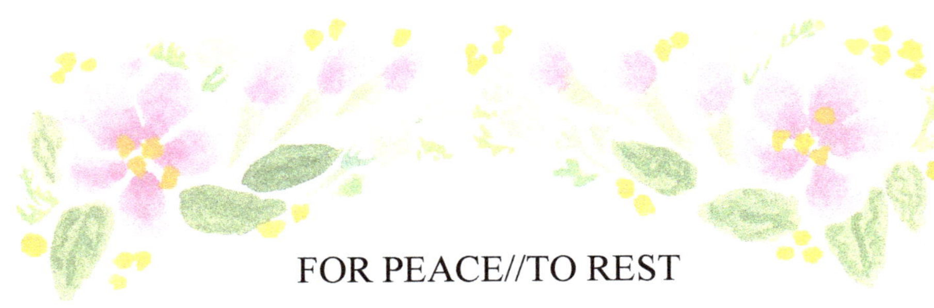

FOR PEACE//TO REST

Clematis:

> *also called traveler's joy*
> *and old man's beard.*
>
> *used to symbolize*
> *ingenuity,*
> *artifice,*
> *and mental beauty.*
>
> *to a wanderer, it may mean rest and safety.*

Queen Anne's Lace:

> *shelter, haven, sanctuary*

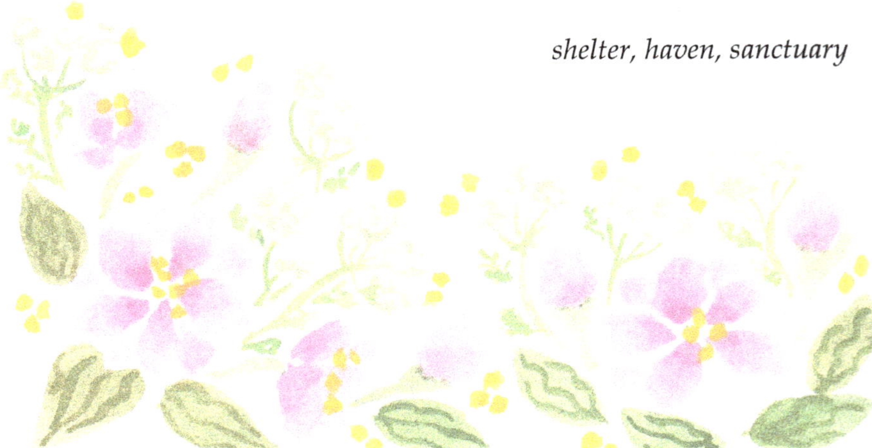

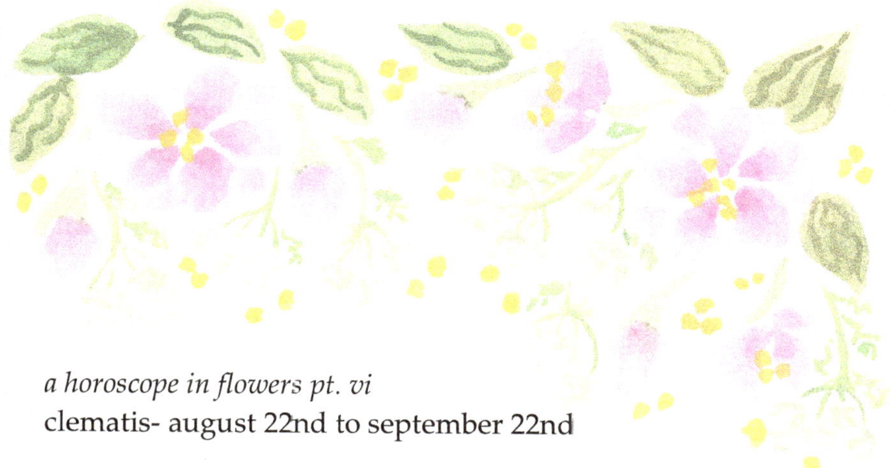

a horoscope in flowers pt. vi
clematis- august 22nd to september 22nd

virgo
your heart is in your hands
cradled gently and carefully
wreathed in flowers to make it prettier and easier to
    consume
the blood leaking from each valve
but you are not for consumption virgo
not to be devoured, even if
the people around you need you
you are full and vibrant and lovely
even in your not lovely moments
breath in, virgo
and breathe out your doubts and fears
your heart is in your hands, but it is yours to give
and yours to choose what to do with

Your lucky numbers are 16, 29, and 33.

Like Honey

The cadence of life has, of late, slowed
not abruptly, nor unkindly
but sweetly
and soft
like honey in a little glass jar
or else
the conifer, whose new pruning has left him
the gently letting out of sap

I know not if it is the Summer heat
the air so heavy and tangible
or the birds, so filled with that life-passion
inextinguishable and apparent
or, more simply, the slowing of my own breathing
that comes with the attentiveness of the soul

Whichever it may be,
I am grateful.

Theo Oliver

painting
a jacaranda tree
with steady strokes
the hurt of the world
lifts from my shoulders

Jackie Chou

you were born of stardust
with galaxies on your tongue
and i see it in your eyes
when they light up at the mention of
something you like or
better yet
someone you love

and i see the galaxies darkest abyss
hiding in your glare
when you lose something dear or
cant seem to care

and yet you dare to tell me
that you see nothing special
you even dare utter such lies
when you know the stars perfectly aligned
to make you
in all your beauty and glory
and i will kiss every freckle down your face
watch them like you do the stars of your world
while i admire mine

OJR

Borage bones

I am having a day
where my bones are not
where they're supposed to be
Or maybe every day
has just become a day
where my skeleton has decided
the fight or flight instinct is faulty;
I am having a day
that I wish wasn't day at all,
but a dark night
where bones are simply tired,
where bones are simply quiet.
I am having a day
where I need courage to manipulate myself
into believing my flesh
belongs to me.
Sometimes I question
what parts of me are real,
but my bones-
I know they're mine.
My bones are scarcely ignored.

Erelah Emerson

Deliver us from evil, we pray
But what if
The evil
Is within us?

Then repent, they say
But what if
The evil
Is only potential?

When what you fear
Is becoming evil
There is no rest
(Wicked or not)

Ziel

FOR HOPE//TO HOPE

Celandine:

> *joys to come*

Crocus:

> *hope.*
> *winter will end*
> *spring will come*
> *life will go on*
> *(always)*

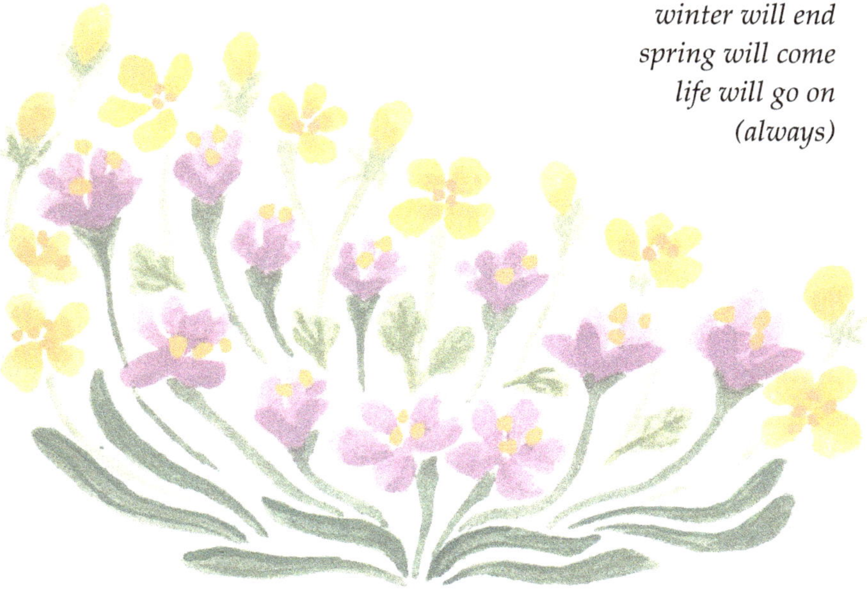

a horoscope in flowers pt. vii
dandelions- september 23rd to october 22nd

libra
always so quick to grow when you can
quick to spread quick to solidify yourself
but your roots are shallow
because you expect to be unearthed so roughly
grow into the dirt, libra
find peace in the rich and dark soil
you are not a weed
as much as you make yourself bitter and tough
did you forget you were a flower too
and that the love you give to others
you have to also receive
take it freely libra
they give out of their hearts
and mean what they say

Your lucky numbers are 23, 14, and 3.

Garden of Self

Dear, this mind I know is unpredictable, bursting in
unprecedented emotions and
Calamitous surges of intrusive notions,
Drowning in oceans – boundless, helpless.
But imagine, think deeply of this spirit, this psyche,
isn't it a garden of myriad
blossoming growths?
A garden resplendent in hope,
This garden slumbers on, maybe
Like droning bees and fallen leaves calling for a rested
autumn sleep
Thickets of crocus grow like mushy bushes
Then this inside might tend to be slushy the myocardium
might crouch on
like a haunch of pain in an unending silence.
But these ribs contain all the power that you own,
The latent seeds of nourishment shall grow as spring comes
again and again,
With hope humming and flashing fast like
the flapping wings of hummingbirds
With the amaranth euphoria of a lovely leather sky
With the dandelion lightness, and daisies of drowsy dreams,
To bring alive faith and promise like the effloresce of lotus,
Intoxicated and purified in zinnia no scent,
This garden, flourishes—evergreen and all your own.

S. Rupsha Mitra

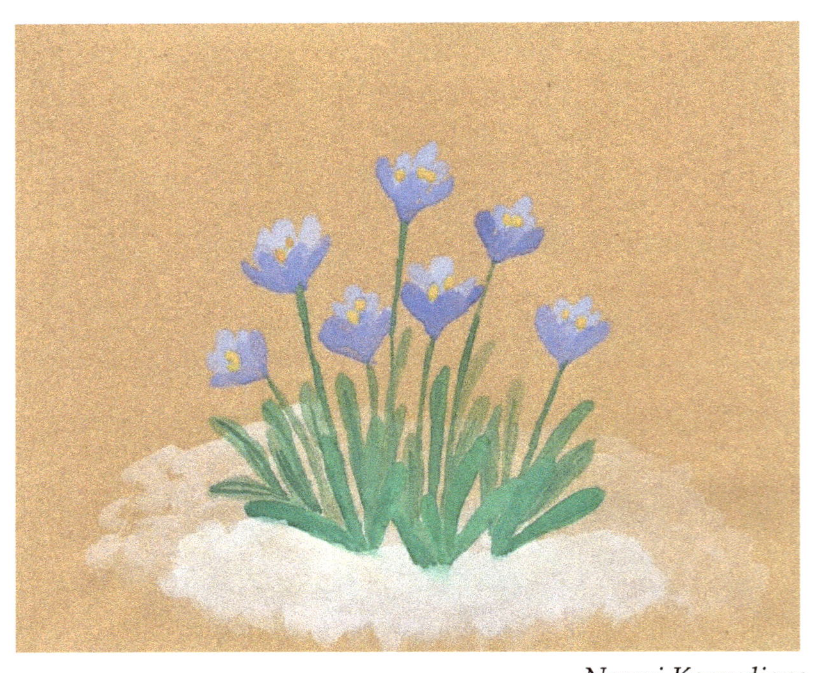

Naomi Karsudjono

Rise

They grow,
in that place some call home.
Nestled between mountains and valleys,
up or down,
tenacity at its finest.
Fragile, yet resilient,
strength of the human spirit.
Out of a cold, dismal winter,
the first to emerge each spring.
A testament to perseverance.
Among the colourless plains,
these purple flowers bloom.
A beacon to those
who need a reminder...
a sense of hope and renewal.
Fail not, they whisper in the wind.
There is light.
Maybe not today, or tomorrow -
but, without a doubt...
there
     is
       light!
For in the darkest hour,
they continue to fight to thrive.
To break the surface.
To be victorious.
Unwilling to give up,
despite the endless snow.
Oh, but to be a prairie crocus, darling!

Becky B.

**Wormwood: A plant that smells so sweet and looks so nice
but will kill you if you take a bite**

Who am I to say that I have been given heavy burdens?
I look like I have the perfect life
From being middle class to attending church
From being at school daily to getting good grades
But daily a cloud hangs over me and lightning fills the sky
My anxiety closes in and my depression weighs me down
And I cannot reach out for a hand to grab
Because
I am
A man

I must be strong; I must be emotionless!
I do not need help!
I do not need friends!
And I do not need a manual on how to live!
I am like Wormwood
Perfect and precious on the outside and death on the inside

Why not jump?
Out the window into the darkness?
A darkness I know all too well,
A darkness I live in alone and cannot escape
70% of suicides are male
And I almost became part of it

An invisible hand
Holds me back

Because no,
This is not the way.
The world needs to change

So, I have picked up my gauntlet
To spread the word
That no man is immune
To emotions and change
A shocking realization
That mental illness affects us all.

Erik Olson

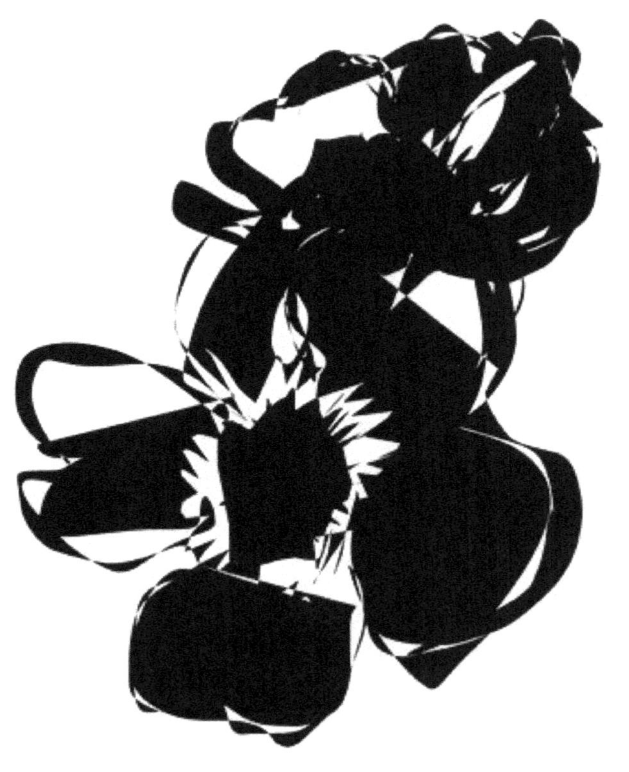

Erelah Emerson

My friend, I wish you heather
I wish you sunlight
I wish you good fortune
I wish you safety

When the darkness closes in
And glowing eyes open
I wish you a breath of fresh air
And a soft bed of purple

And a promise that
Someday
Somehow
Spring will come again

Ziel

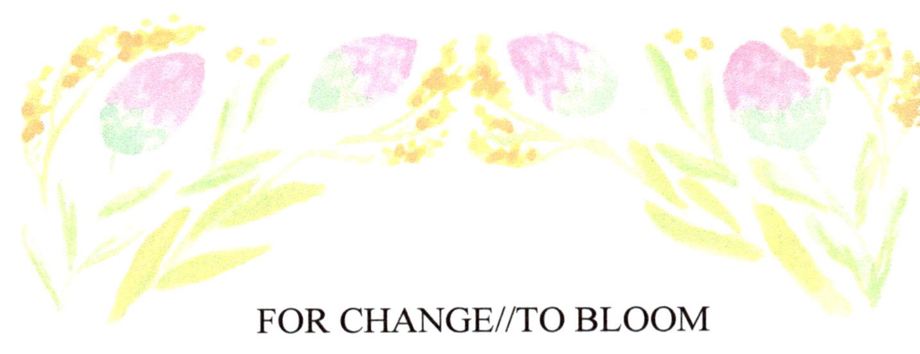

FOR CHANGE//TO BLOOM

Goldenrod:

encouragement,
growth,
support

Protea:

diversity,
transformation,
courage.

Lotus:

rebirth

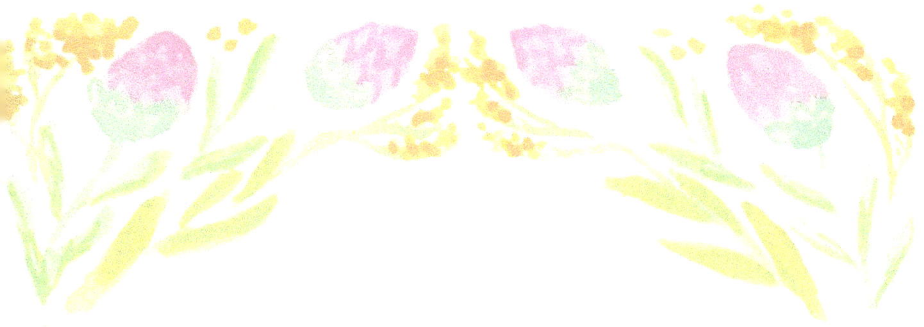

a horoscope in flowers pt. viii
thistle- october 23rd to november 22nd

scorpio
you have buried yourself in the soft pink spike of protection
so guarded that no one can hurt you
no one can help you either
but that doesn't matter to you
because you are safe
and that is a noble goal, but
we miss you scorpio
miss your wit and your company
so if you could
would you come join us
gently and patiently as we wait with bated breath

Your lucky numbers are 13, 96, and 81.

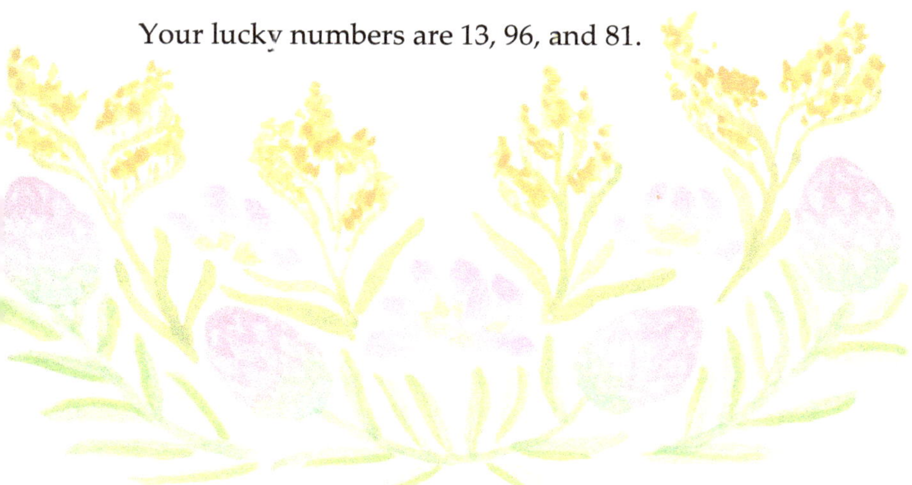

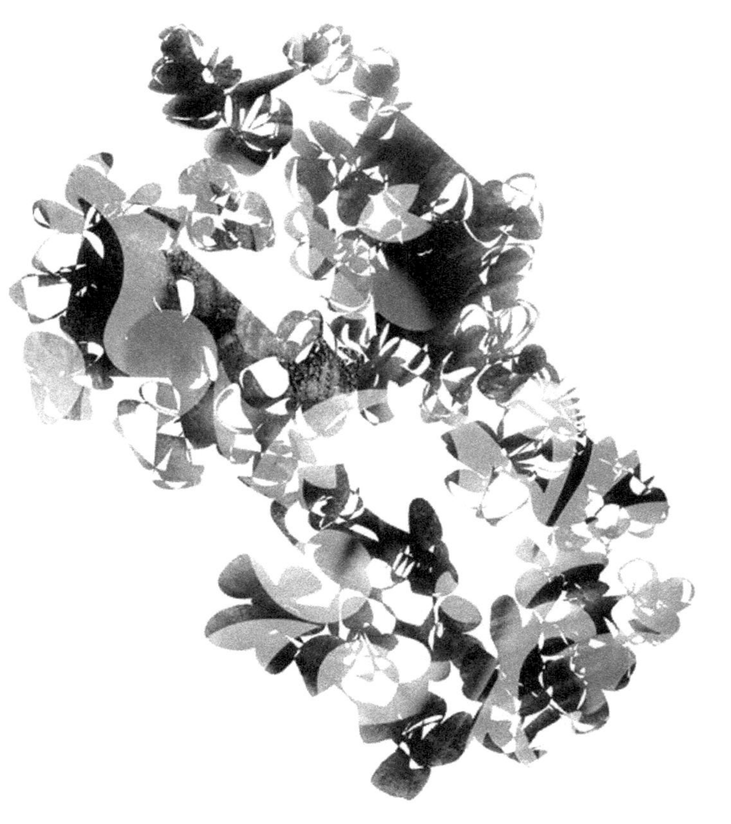

Erelah Emerson

Something New

This summer I have gone outside
and tanned in the sun
And that is something new
New like a lover
New like trusting
New like staying still
Unflinching as the bees bumble past me to the heather
To the coriander, to the thyme
To the garden on the porch that is still beautiful
Even the half of it that's not for me
(I am learning to be okay with that)
This summer
The heat knocks me down, but not out
My bed claims me
But not as often as i leave it
I curl my fists around opportunity
And the monster on my shoulders stills and trusts my
    judgment
I whisper that I want, *i want*
for the first time in my life I want
And the beast at my center nods
And asks first before it holds me tight.
This summer
I am a little bit well
(Praise God, at last)
I am better and worse
I am trying, learning, reaching for a l i v e
(Praise God, my God at last)

SJ Blasko

There are 2 things you must know:

1. Sometimes he will come back and sometimes even heavier
   than before but I need you to never forget that each year
   he comes,

His visits get shorter.
Each year he yells a little quieter
And one day,
He will lose his set of keys and never come back.
One day you won't have to keep changing all the locks
Because one day
He just won't come.
And one day will turn into a year
And one year will turn into opening the windows and
   drawing the blinds.
One year will turn into thanking the key master down the
   street for being so patient with all your visits
And thanking the mailman for fitting two weeks' worth of
   mail into your mailbox because you went days without
   leaving your house.
One year will turn into your life
That you took back from your illness,
From that voice.
You won't hear him yell anymore.
You won't have to change the locks
And

2. If he ever does come back,
You will know that just became you hear him does not mean
   you have to listen.

- November
  Kath Kane

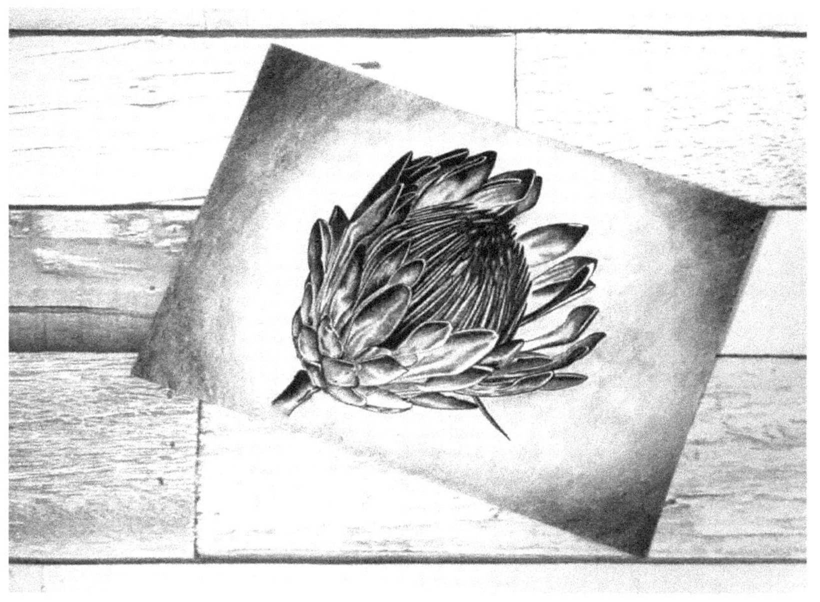

Sarah Birch

The Silver Lining

Wrapped up in my blanket, I lay on my bed.
The clock's ticking sound reminded me of each passing
second.
And my beating heart reminded me of my existence,
An existence, the burden of which was slowly becoming
unbearable.
With each beat I was flooded with the agonizing memories of
my life,
The failures, the deceits, the past abusive relationship. . .
My life suddenly felt redundant.
All I wanted was to close my eyes and slowly transcend to a
different world.
This physical world was too bad to live in.
My heart ached. A terrible pain had immersed every muscle,
every organ and every bone of my body.
Endless tears and sleepless nights,
This pain had become integrally intertwined with my
existence.

I closed my eyes, and I could hear their voices.
My ex-boyfriend calling me a whore,
My mother crying over my father's business losses,
My professor constantly harassing me mentally,
My friends calling me names behind my back. . .
I was a failure; I was a loser.
Outside I could hear the DJ playing some grooving tracks,
The festival was on and people were going crazy.
And here I suffered, crying again over my life that had gone
astray.

I looked at the strip of sleeping pills.
The psychiatrist had prescribed them.
I was depressed, he said, and I needed to sleep.
Nothing had helped.
Even after a month of counseling sessions with the
psychiatrist and psychologist, the pain remained.
I still felt as helpless as before.
I wanted to thrash my head on the wall,
I wanted to jump off the fifth floor of my hostel,
I wanted to cut my heart out and burn it into ashes,
I wanted my body to just perish,
I wanted to get rid of this pain,
I wanted my normal life back,
But ah! The pain just wouldn't leave my ailing body.
I looked at myself in the mirror,
I had become a pale shadow of my former self,
I saw pity on the face the mirror reflected,
This couldn't go on anymore,
I could not endure anymore,
I took the strip of sleeping pills,
One,
Two,
Three,
Knock! Knock!
Four,
Knock! Knock!
Five,
Knock! Knock!
I stopped gulping the pills to attend to the irritating knocks
at my door,
I opened the door and fainted.

All I remember was my friends surrounding me, crying.
They took away all the strips of pills while I retired to bed, in
my head, all the while, cursing them!
The thought of a new day terrified me. . .

Outside the counseling center my boyfriend was waiting for
me, with tears in his eyes and with a tub that had a small
seedling.
He held me in his arms, but my heart was cold and
unresponsive.
I felt nothing until I found myself in tears again.
We spent the entire night staring sightlessly at the starry sky
and when the sun dawned we departed with a promise,
He wanted me to take care of the seedling and I hollowly
agreed.
I placed the tub on my balcony and slept.

The counseling sessions continued; my counselor was
desperately trying to help me open up,
I had lost all hopes of living a normal life again,
And somehow, callous people showed the audacity to say
that I was pretending to be depressed
that there was no such thing as depression,
I was being judged. I was being cornered, even by my
friends.

One morning I found that roots had begun to shoot out from
the seed,
A peculiar wave of happiness ran through my nerves,
I immediately started watering the seedling,
And a week thereafter came the first tiny leaf!

I was thrilled beyond my wits,
For the first time in months I felt a hope slowly glimmering
in my eyes,
With each passing day, the counselor sensed a slow yet
steady change,
I was smiling,
I was joining my friends in their conversations,
I was even having proper meals at proper times!
And at the end of each day I would find myself clinging to
the seedling that had now grown into a sapling,
I would talk with it constantly,
Sometimes I would sing to it,
Sometimes I would just sit beside it and let the silence soothe
me,
It was as if a part of me was growing with it every day.

A month passed.
A small bud had taken birth, and my happiness knew no
bounds.
As the plant danced in the air, I could feel a rush of
adrenaline in my body,
My scars were healing, my heart too!
That day I laughed my heart out in front of my counselor,
She was crying, she had never expected that from a charred
soul like mine.
She held my hand and told me I had a warrior spirit, it had
just been lying low
like a dormant volcano

Finally, the last counseling session.

I woke up with a renewed enthusiasm and opened the door
of the balcony.
There, with its head towards the sun like a king, stood a
sunflower,
A blooming, bright-yellow sunflower!
All these days I had nurtured the seedling like a baby
Not knowing that the fruit would be so amazingly beautiful!
As I thanked my therapist and bid adieu to the counseling
center, I walked out on the road with my head held high,
aiming for the skies.
I had risen up from my ashes like a phoenix, and a new life
beckoned me now.
I had shirked off the barbed clothes of depression,
abandonment anxiety, panic attacks.
I was now adorned with a new-found confidence; a new-
found love for this life that God has endowed me with.
As I hugged my boyfriend, I thanked him a billion times for
changing my life.
The baby seed had managed to spread the roots of optimism
and hope in my life,
With each baby step the seedling took towards full bloom,
my heart took the plunge too,
The desire to transform my life for the better steadily rooted
in my heart,
The birth of one tiny leaf had sent shivers down my spine.
I was slowly rediscovering myself.
I was slowly falling in love with my scars, my wounded
heart, my once abused body, my pain, my vulnerabilities, my
excessive emotions. . . everything belonged to me,
I might be messy, chaotic, yet I am beautiful because I exist.

While I walked towards my favorite tea-shop, hand in hand
with my boyfriend, the image of the blooming sunflower
flashed in front of my eyes,
It reminded me of how precious this life is,
I had struggled my way through the darkest nights, but they
were over now,
The sunflower symbolized my rebirth.
The sunflower was my silver lining.

Somjeeta Pandey

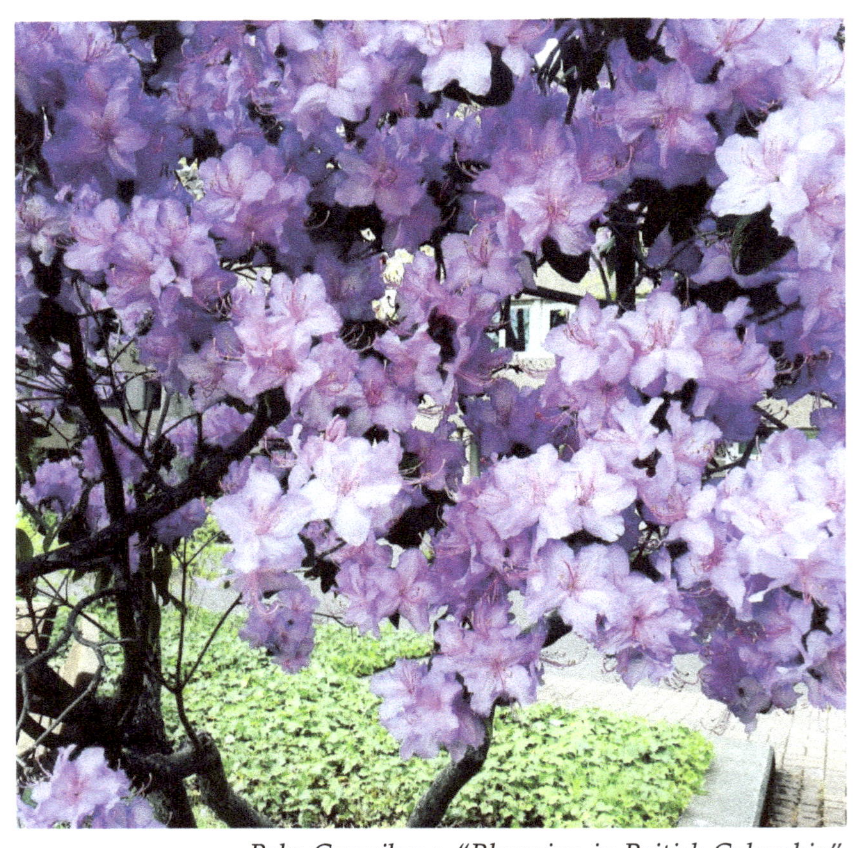

Beka Gremikova, "Blooming in British Columbia"

catching raining blossoms
with open hands

how free
this dance in the wind

that blew him away

Jackie Chou

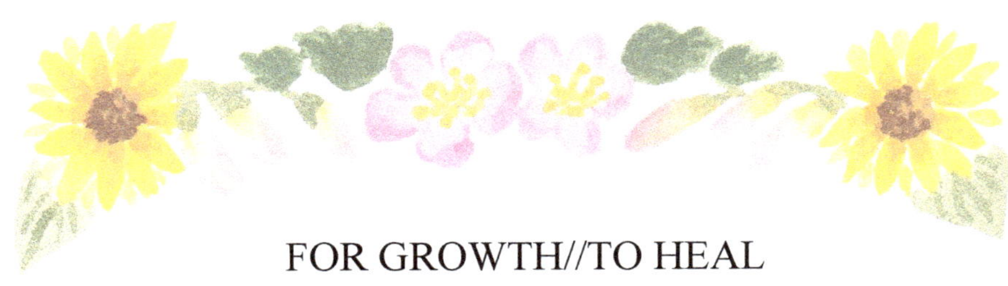

FOR GROWTH//TO HEAL

Eglantine:

"a wound to heal"

Plumeria:

new beginnings,
birth and creation,
shelter and protection

Sunflowers:

a common symbol among those with depression.
represents lifting your face to the sun.

light. hope. joy.
things will get better.

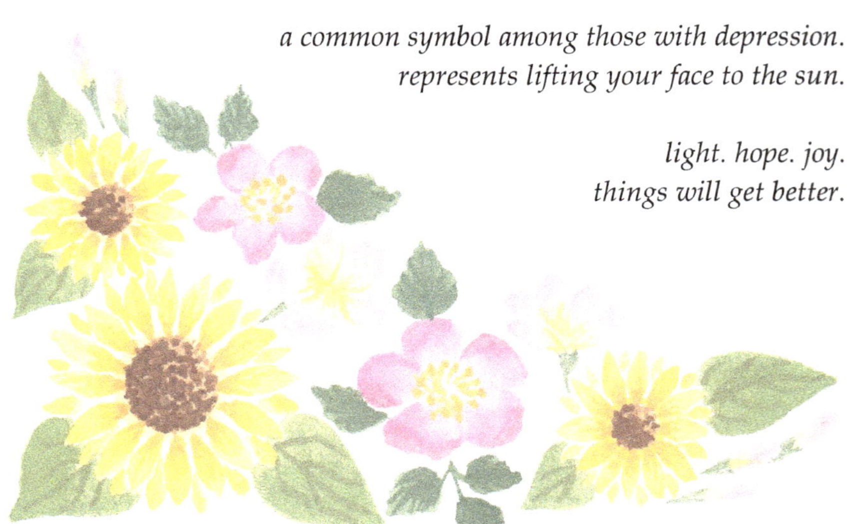

a horoscope in flowers pt. ix
sunflower- november 23rd to december 21st

steady and strong
sagittarius you are a firm ground to jump off of
a gentle place to land
growing tall and yellow and beautiful
wonderful to look at and gentle to touch
petals like gentle kisses
leaves big and wide enough to touch the sky
you will be alright sagittarius
and the yellowness of your light will reach the furthest
    corner
and we will heal. and we will heal. and we will heal.

Your lucky numbers are 27, 15, and 64.

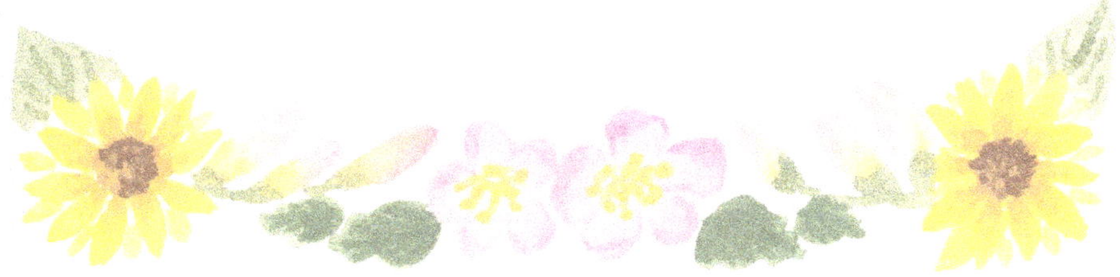

141

The Face of the Earth

The water ran down the cobblestone path, rushing past the broken fountain and continuing on its way into the depths of the woods. I followed its wild trail beyond the borders of the cottage, where the trees ran wild and the ground split with hunger. The cries of the earth, once weak and empty, howled loud in my ears as I leaped over the tiny crevices. I walked between the bowing trees and pushed through a gaping hole in a thick wall of vines. It was here that I found her, a small girl who sat with her hands buried in the dirt. Beneath her legs, the grass was long and withered, the ends blackened like they had been playing with fire. Her eyes were closed and she mumbled incoherent words in the privacy of her head.

I felt as though I had broken into something I wasn't supposed to see. I sat down and stared, waiting for her to acknowledge me. She waited beneath the sun's cycle until it had vanished, leaving the moon to take over its jealous sky. Her eyes opened and looked at me with a sense of shock and curiosity. She slowly pulled her hands from the ground and crossed them in her lap. Like the grass, their ends were black and they looked like they would soon crack.

"Who are you?" I asked plainly, leaning forward while she stared.

Her mouth opened slowly and she tried to speak but her words weren't used to being heard. They hid in the back of her throat until she forced them out. "I'm Fayre."

"I'm Pynt." I stuck out my hand, politely like my mother
had taught me, until I realized that her blackened hands
weren't going to touch mine. I tucked them in my lap and
looked around. "Where are we? I know these woods more
than most, but I've never been here before."

She looked behind me. I followed her gaze, staring at the
thick wall of vines that was supposed to separate her from
the world. The gaping hole where I'd climbed through
wasn't supposed to be there. I could see that now, as plainly
as I could tell when it was day. The rest of the wall was so
tightly grown that no one would be able to get through it.

"No one is supposed to find me." She winced, pushing her
hands back into the earth and closing her eyes again. This
time it was only for a second. "Your world is dying and I
seem to be the only one who can save it."

She brushed back her hair, sweat beading on her forehead.

I shuffled closer and placed my hand on the dirt. It pulled,
burying my fingers in the soil, connecting me to the roots of
the earth. I could feel it straining, pulling on my energy,
burning as it carried throughout my body. I gasped in pain
and pulled back.

"You can feel it too." She looked at me with bewilderment
and wonder. "I have been doing this for weeks, trying to
save you all."

I took her hand. It was ruined and would never fully heal
but she wasn't too far gone. "Sometimes you have to let

others save themselves. You can't be expected to place the world on your shoulders just because they can't see the problems around them."

"But if I take my hands away they might all die."

"Or they will see what is happening and do their part to fix it." I pulled her from the small alcove, leading her back into the woods. I could feel the ground shaking, the world groaning in protest as we chose to abandon it. We could not hold the burdens on our backs so we left them in order to find our own way, revealing the world to the innocent so that they could bear their own weight.

Nathaniel Luscombe

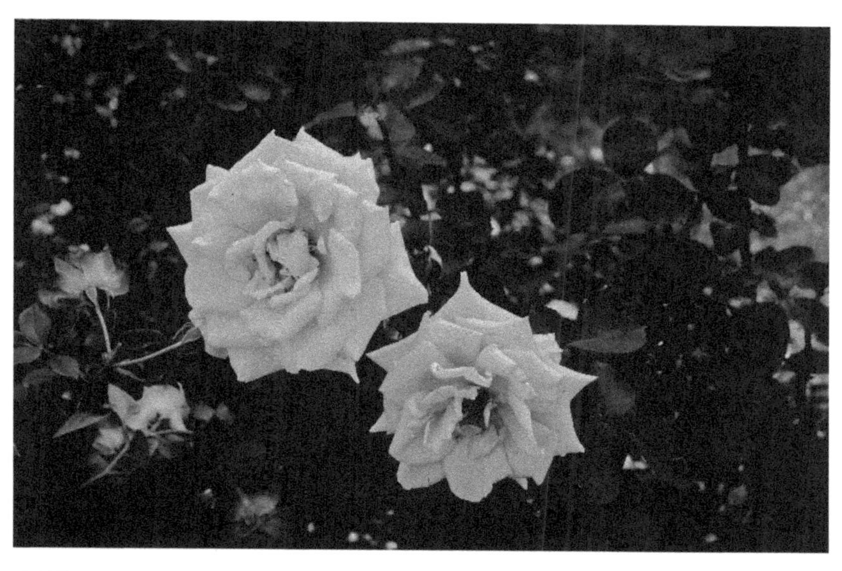

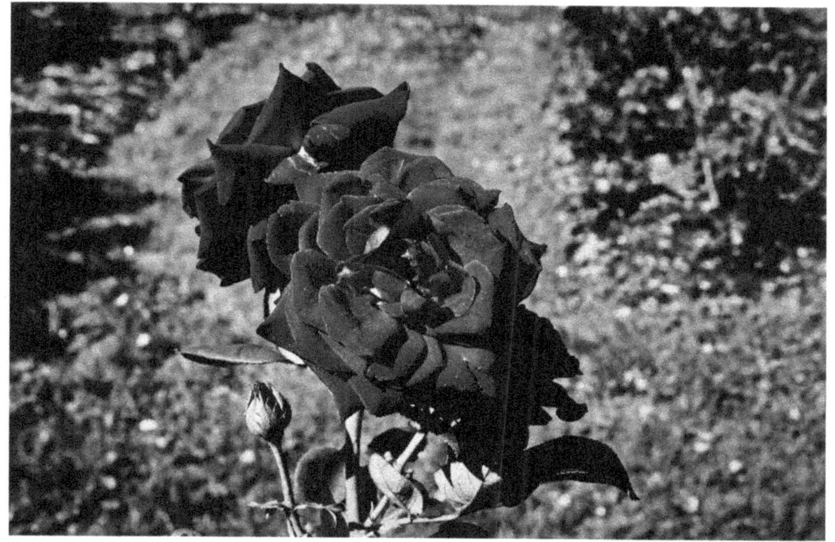

Naomi Slingerland

before you, I picked thorn covered roses; begging them to
be a distraction from the numbness that filled my life.
everyday was static, such silence it hurt. while pleading for
the light to appear at the end of my tunnel, I found you.

wind whistled around you— your silhouette beamed; at
that moment, I knew you were the light I called for. your
laugh, it finally broke the silence. and it was euphoric. I
needed more— I needed to be engulfed in it.
you showed me the innocence of life, the softness of your
words finally made the roses dethorn. I allowed them to wilt.

you help me feel how cherry blossoms look: pure petals
and innocent pinks, the wind makes the flowers dance.

pink never fit into my world until you walked in; now,
pink means purity and softness, innocent kisses before bed.
our aura's dance within the bright lights of our kitchen, all
while the aroma of pancakes fill the air.
I want to lie in it, forever.

—gardens can always be renovated.

Kimmy Renee

Rosemary

You're allergic to rosemary.
It makes your eyes water and throat itchy.
My eyes water and my throat prickles
Late at night when you aren't by my side
Maybe
I'm allergic to being alone.

Loneliness.
It's amazing how easily you destroy it
Little jokes on the phone and gentle words
Every bit of anxiety vanishes in your arms
Love is healing my fragile wounds
And warms me to the core

OJR

Dandelions

Sweat glistens on the fingertips that fiddle with the hem of my tank top.

My other, restless hand sweeps my soft, chopped hair behind my ears. I repeat the motion, tucking it in again, harder. Never satisfied the strands will stay in place.

At the front of my skull, there's a dull, throbbing pounding, almost loud enough to drown out Tyler's voice.

"Jackson said he'd try to bring Katrina to the barbeque— she was supposed to have a shift at the hospital this afternoon, but I think she got off." Tyler's fingers drum the steering wheel: a calm rhythm. Nothing like my desperate fidgeting. My sheen of sweat.

Tyler eases the truck towards a stop sign with steady pressure on the brakes. "Even if Katrina's not there, Jackson will be. Anytime there's a barbeque at Nicki's place, you'd have to lock Jackson in the basement to keep him away from those ribs and that coleslaw."

Tyler chuckles at his own joke. When I don't laugh along, he swivels to face me, bright summer sun glinting off his square crew cut. His strong, shaven jaw.

"Sasha, you feeling okay?"

My hand strays to my bobbed haircut again, a classic tell for my social anxiety which Tyler, three weeks into our relationship, hasn't yet identified.

I manage a straight smile. No wobbles. I only repeat myself once when I speak, which must be a new record. "I'm—I'm fine."

"You're pretty quiet," Tyler grunts, as he catches my fluttery hand in his own for a squeeze. Warm. Solid. I do my best to focus on his grip, clinging like a swimmer to a rock. Tyler strokes his thumb across my knuckles. My heartbeat slows.

"You're not scared of this party, are you?" He's driving with one hand, his eyes zigzagging between me and the road. He sounds genuinely concerned, but I don't dare trust that. I shake my head.

"If you *were* scared, you know I'd protect you, right?" Tyler raises one eyebrow. His lips press together, and like the flip of a switch, I sense the Army training kicking in. The training that sees fear in concrete, real-world terms: threats to eliminate. Bad guys to take down.

Not dark shadows of my brain's own making.

He wouldn't understand. I need him to think I'm fine.

I need him to think I'm *normal*.

"Sasha?"

His arm slides around my shoulders. I've got to do a better job of acting. I breathe out a giggle, lean back into the softness. His arm tightens, because he likes that. I cut a sideways glance at him through my wisps of dark hair, because Tyler likes that, too.

"How would you protect me?" I grin—and the grin is only partly fake.

"Kill a guy," Tyler says, his mouth twitching. "No big deal."

I snort. "You'd go to jail!"

"Not if I grow a beard and drive to Canada."

My laugh hitches in my side. It hurts, but a good hurt— not like the anxious ache in my skull. "Please, no! Don't grow a beard!"

"Would you leave me if I grew a beard?" Tyler leans over and kisses the top of my head, a quick, fierce touch.

I'm giggling too hard to answer, my worries all but forgotten . . . when, without warning, the truck slides to a halt.

I sit up straight. Fingers automatically twisting my shirt. "Wait, we're here already?"

Blood pounds my eardrums, muting Tyler's reply, as I gaze through the fly-spattered windshield with mounting terror. We're parked at the end of the neighborhood block.

Ahead of us stretch a dozen vehicles, maybe more, their chipped paint baking in the afternoon heat. The long trail leads straight to a tiny pink stucco house, with tell-tale blue barbeque smoke wafting from the back porch. *Nicki's place*, I know without asking. Even from here, I can see how the yard crawls with people. Bursts with humans.

My limbs go heavy.

I duck my head, fumble at my seatbelt buckle. I *will* make my fingers work. I will make my legs work.

The passenger door swings open, and Tyler's voice rumbles through. "Sasha, baby, you ready?"

"Yes," I mumble. My throat feels oddly tight, pressing inward.

Breathe, idiot.

One shoe, then the other, manages to touch solid sidewalk. I grab Tyler's hand like a lifeline. I try so, so, so hard not to look, but I can't help it. My glance snags the line of cars once more—and just like that, the last bit of oxygen leaks from my lungs.

Light-headed . . .

Chest pain . . .

Bent over double . . .

Oh, this is not happening.

Not here, my soul screams at whoever controls the universe. *Not in front of Tyler.*

"Sasha!"

Everything goes black, blurry. I can't see him. I can't see anything. My whole world is shaking. Shuddering. Knives stab me, rip me open with each frantic gasp for air. I will suffocate. I will drown. Drown, and die, and never get a chance to explain that I'm not—I'm not—I'm not—

"Baby, what's wrong? Talk to me!"

I'm not a freak—

Through the fog, I begin to feel a few things outside of myself. Tyler's hands gripping my bare shoulders. Cold palms against hot skin. I'm fevered, sweaty. Tyler pulling me upright, pushing me against the solid metal of the truck. The paint's dim warmth through my faded jeans. I'm a furnace inside, and nothing else can compete.

"Sasha." Tyler cups my chin. I squeeze my eyes shut: duck the shame of looking him in the face. "Sasha, can you talk? Can you hear me?"

I swallow, tasting bitter adrenaline on my tongue. My throat is still glued shut. Besides, I have no breath left to speak.

"Sasha, if you don't answer, I swear to God I'm calling 911."

My eyes are still closed, but my fingers find the tattoo on his forearm, even without looking. I trace the darkened ink, smoky reds and whites and blues.

When it finally comes, it's just a whisper.

"I'm sorry, Tyler."

He exhales in a rush. Like I said the wrong thing. *"Sasha."*

Panic blocks my chest once more, pumps blood to my brain. "I'm—I'm s-sorry—"

"Baby, don't." His jaw snaps, grimly, but his hug closes around me. Shielding me. Soaking up my tremors. His other arm reaches past, and I hear the groan of the passenger door swinging wide. Before I know what's going on, he boosts me back into my seat . . . guides my fingers to find the seatbelt . . .

"We're not l-leaving?" I gulp.

No, no. This is bad. All my life, this has been a bad sign. The sign that my panic attacks have ruined everything, and I'm about to be punished.

"Sasha, don't worry about it." That's the last I hear of Tyler's voice, before he slams the door shut. Through the stained windshield, his head bobs with long, angry strides, making his way around to the driver's side.

My stomach flips. When Tyler slides into the seat beside me, a flood of speech tumbles out. "I'm sorry, I really am! I know it's stupid, I didn't mean to—"

"You still think I'm mad at you?" He turns, his eyebrows crumpled together. His forehead a row of dark lines, all the way up to the close-shaved hair. "Sasha, what kind of jerk do you take me for?"

I shrink back into the seat cushions. "Um."

"Okay, don't answer that. I'm screwing this up, aren't I. Nice job, Tyler." He exhales again, before finding my hand and cradling it on his knee. "Let's take a little drive, baby. You and me."

I don't have the energy left to explain why this is a bad idea. Tyler turns the key in the ignition and brings the engine spluttering, roaring to life.

"I . . . I don't think I can drink coffee," I quaver, as the green-and-white Starbucks sign shoves into view through our windshield.

"I'm not getting you coffee." Tyler brings the truck to a halt in one of the curbside spots, jumps to the pavement, and disappears into the store.

I close my eyes, tears pricking the lids. The worst of my trembling has died away, but one stubborn little shiver buries itself deep in my stomach. I feel wrung out, limp. Like a wet mitten lost in the melting snow.

I know I need to ground myself. I touch the vinyl cracks of the seat bottom and find the pinkish, fuzzy fiber poking out. I crank the window halfway down, breathe the shimmery summer heat. I run my hands through my messy hair, teasing out the tangles, one by one. I peer through the windshield at the curb. Creeper grass bursts upward, hungry, exuberant. Dandelions nod their yellow lion manes.

But immune to distractions, the memories still play, over and over,

"Freak."

"Sissy."

"Acting out."

"She just wants attention. Don't reward her."

And little Sasha, hiding behind her bangs, fidgeting with her clothes; watching the show play out. A never-ending circus, where she's the resident freak in the big tent. Five years old, first grade, second grade. Middle school, senior year, first job. Foster homes, friends' couches, boyfriends' apartments. No matter how old she gets, no matter how many episodes she survives, no one believes her when she says, *"My head hurts."*

"Sasha. Hey."

Jolted back to the present, I blink at Tyler, my throat too rocky to form an answer.

Tyler leans closer, scanning my face. The skin around his eyes strains tight. His jaw muscles lump up. He clears his throat a few times before he says, "Here, Sasha. Brought you something to drink."

"Oh." Startled, my gaze drops to his hands for the first time. He's holding a clear plastic cup with a perky green straw sticking upwards. It's full to the brim with water, ice cubes bouncing near the top.

"Thank—thank you," I mumble. My palms close around it.

Just balancing the cup in my lap calms me. I feel its chilled, substantial weight. Cold droplets form on the plastic and rub off onto my fingers. I bring the straw to my lips, and serenity gushes into my mouth.

Ice water.

How did Tyler guess?

He waits for me to take a long drink, lowering the water level in the cup by a few centimeters. He strokes my hair behind my ears, smooths it gently. Fingers a few loose, dark strands.

When the cool liquid reaches my stomach, washing away that last, lingering tremor, Tyler's voice breaks the silence.

"So, you had a panic attack."

"A panic attack?" I swipe aside my bangs to see him clearly, my eyes swelling like saucers. "You—know about my panic attacks?"

One corner of his mouth quirks. "Uh, I do *now*?"

"No, but, I mean." My brain flounders, hearing my boyfriend so easily drop a phrase only my state-mandated therapists have ever used. "How did you learn about panic attacks?"

"PTSD," Tyler says without hesitation. He shrugs, fingers lightly drumming the infantry tattoo on his arm. "Plenty of my buddies get 'em since coming back."

"Oh," is all I can respond.

I duck my gaze and take another cold sip. When I venture upwards again, Tyler is looking directly at me.

"Do you have PTSD, Sasha?"

I would give everything I have to escape this moment. To melt away, mist away into the bright blue sky, a dream world where no one is broken, where nothing hurts. I stare fixedly at the strong slanting beams of sunshine; willing myself the strength to speak clearly, at least, if I can't will myself invisible. But only Tyler's touch on my cheek is enough to bring out the words.

"I have . . . social anxiety disorder."

"Social anxiety disorder," he repeats, his knuckles a warm presence against my jaw. He hasn't jerked his hand away. He hasn't started yelling about how I tricked him into dating a psycho. He hasn't done, well, anything that should scare me.

So why does my heart hammer my ribs?

Tyler seems to sense the rising fear, because he wraps an arm across my shoulders. "Social anxiety, huh? You see some kind of therapist for that?"

I lean into his hug, going through the motions of a normal conversation. Praying this will *stay* a normal conversation, not erupt into a fight. I try to string my voice along at a normal pace. "Not since foster care ended and the state stopped paying for it." Deep breath. "I, um, the money—"

Tyler interrupts. Numbers always get his attention. "You're twenty-three and you've been without therapy for five years?" He twists sharply. "Sasha, no wonder you're—"

"Such a freak?"

I don't mean to spit those words out, but out they come, fierce and quivering. Acid pulses through my veins. Everything burns. Everything fizzes. Everything tastes sour, bitter.

Then I realize what I've done, and the panic floods back in.

"I'm sorry," I gasp.

I can't look at him, but I hear the squeaking noise of sticky vinyl, as Tyler scoots along the connected seat towards me. Casually, he relieves me of the Starbucks cup, plunking it down on the dashboard. Then he drags me into his lap, completely crushing me in his strong arms.

My nose squashes on his shoulder. Despite everything, I almost giggle. As I squirm around, repositioning myself, my head finds the hollow between Tyler's neck and shoulder, and nestles there.

"That's better," Tyler announces. He plants a kiss on my cheek. When I giggle, for real this time, more kisses land on the same spot.

"Baby," he nuzzles my neck, "believe it or not, I was never gonna call you a freak."

I keep hiding in the safety of his chest. I don't trust myself to pull back and let him look at me just yet. "Thanks . . . thanks."

"I was only gonna say," Tyler goes on, one hand cupped over the arch of my spine, "there's some battles it's not the best strategy to fight alone."

I nod against him. "You're right. I know."

He ruffles my hair. "I'll help you cover therapy."

I snap upright, wiping stray tears from my eyelashes. "*Excuse* me!"

"Aw, get off your high horse," Tyler flashes a grin. "If I can buy you dinner, I can buy you therapy."

Laughter bubbles up inside me, but I put my head on one side, lips pressed sternly together. "Excuse ME."

Tyler's on a roll now, greenish eyes twinkling as he teases. "If I can buy you makeup, I can buy you therapy . . ."

"Who says you can buy me makeup?"

"If I can work on your car when it breaks down—and trust me, baby, it *will* break down, that thing's a piece of trash on wheels if I ever saw one—then I can buy you therapy—"

I punch him in the ribs, shrieking, laughing. He dives in for a quick kiss that melts into a longer kiss, his lips soft against my shy ones. I feel myself flush pink.

When I break away, Tyler's eyes follow me in a way that turns my cheeks even redder, but still, I'm grinning. He chuckles, a happy sound.

I ease off his lap and into my own seat. Tyler settles under the steering wheel. Before I can reach the ice water, he hands the cup to me. I clutch its damp, slick sides, and try to make my question sound unconcerned.

"Should we, um, go back to the barbeque now?"

Tyler rolls his shoulders back, stretching his joints. He glances across. "That's up to you, Sasha."

My gulp sounds pretty obvious, despite my efforts. "Up to—me?"

"Sasha, I'm not taking you someplace you don't feel safe. You had a panic attack the minute you saw the house." His hand blankets mine, wrapping it warmly. "How you feeling now? Think you can handle it?"

I shift against the seat back. Dark, ugly words, the ghosts of people long gone, rise up to haunt me.

"If I say 'no,'" I whisper into the silence, "will you tell me I've ruined everything?"

"Ruined everything?"

Tyler snorts.

"Nah, I'll text Nicki to tell her the gang will just have to meet you some other time . . . then I'll take you to a boring movie and kiss you in the dark when things gets too slow."

Relief gushes through me. "Oh."

Tyler wriggles his eyebrows. "If I pick a *really* slow movie, then I get to kiss you *a lot*."

I pinch his tattoo, my laugh breathless. "Shut up!"

"Seriously, Sasha, it's up to you. Whatever you decide, party or no party." He looks me dead in the eyes. His jaw clamps solid, the way it does when he feels something deeply. "I just want you to be safe."

I lower my eyes to our intertwined fingers.

Tyler speaks gently. "What do you want, Sasha?"

In the quiet, I weigh my options.

Through the windshield, the dandelions in the grass catch my gaze once more. I wonder if there's a reason why I've always felt drawn to dandelions. Furry and golden, scraggly, undernourished: but unashamed of who they are. They thrive in life's toughest soil, and turn their faces to the sun.

Trembling a little, but with a firm lift of my chin, I turn back to the man who just gave me the courage to say,

"I want . . ."

Katie Hanna

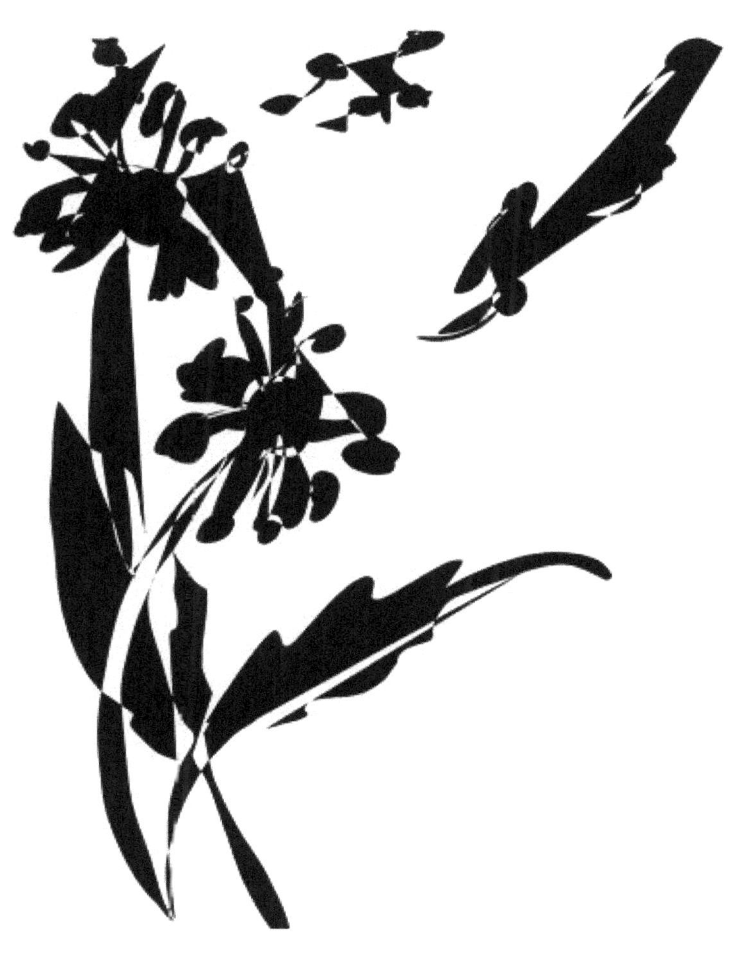

Erelah Emerson

The last time I remember growing,
I remember competing with the trees
and the grass
and the house being built next door.
I remember being envious of the rose bush outside my
     apartment because it always bloomed faster than I ever
     could
and loving the cactus in my room because in comparison,
I was always brimming with growth.
I don't remember when I stopped and learned that growth is
     not a competition.
One day I realized the cactus in my room is not weak for
     growing slowly but strong for thriving from nothing.
One day I realized that to juxtapose myself to a bed of roses
     is to only allow myself 6-8 weeks of blooming.
One day I realized that growth is not linear and that even
     vines creep their way across buildings, sideways and
     upwards and downwards, and still call it progress.
I am still learning that growth comes in different forms and
     moves in different directions and that its intentions are
     never constant.
...
No one ever talks about vines
And how they swallow entire homes
And make it look like growth.

Kath Kane

Zinnia

With a shivering body, Zinnia stands in front of the
    counseling center.
All these years, she has proudly donned the façade of
    happiness on her lips and her dark brown eyes have
    never been allowed to shed a single tear.
She has endured all the harsh sunrises and sunsets, just like a
    zinnia does.
Alone and aloof in a corner, she would silently watch her
    mother go to sleep with hunger roaring like a lion in her
    belly,
Her father, drunk, would keep hurling slurs.

On the day she left home, her mother had reminded her why
    she was named after a flower,
Zinnia, the world outside is filled with raucous men,
You, my child, are a woman, learn to endure.
So she has.
The man she fell in love with was a chivalrous man,
But he body-shamed her and kept abusing her till she broke
    down.
Chivalry, he believed, stemmed from the ability to dominate
    women.
So he did.
He tried to wither her soul and perish her entity.
But he failed to extinguish her spirit.
Zinnia was a survivor, one who could stubbornly survive
    any lows of life.

With a shattered-yet-not-broken-heart and her trembling
    hands carrying a bunch of dandelions, Zinnia takes her
    steps towards the counseling center.

Somjeeta Pandey

I Will Never Walk That Path Again.

In the land of hope, wildflowers grow and are mowed down
	in veins.
There's implied violence in the concept of growth- to destroy
	is to become.
We walk beside the heartsick paths. Refuse to step foot back
	into that darkness again.
And they labelled us common,
As we lived amongst gods.

Eddie L. House

Prescribed Burning

the thing that people don't tell you about wildflowers
is that if you don't burn them back
they will grow over your hands and feet
cling to you and hold you down
sprout over your mouth and fill it
with beautiful petals that choke you out
so pretty to look at
(no one really cares about the lungs of pretty things)
sometimes people will give you flames
to burn away bits and pieces of the wildflowers
to grow their own instead
cactus flowers and red anemones and dead lilies
wilting you from the inside out
let your own fire out my love
curb their flowers and free yourself
keep the wildflowers out of your throat
you are not burning every field
by turning a handful of invasive flowers to ash

Adrien Farinas

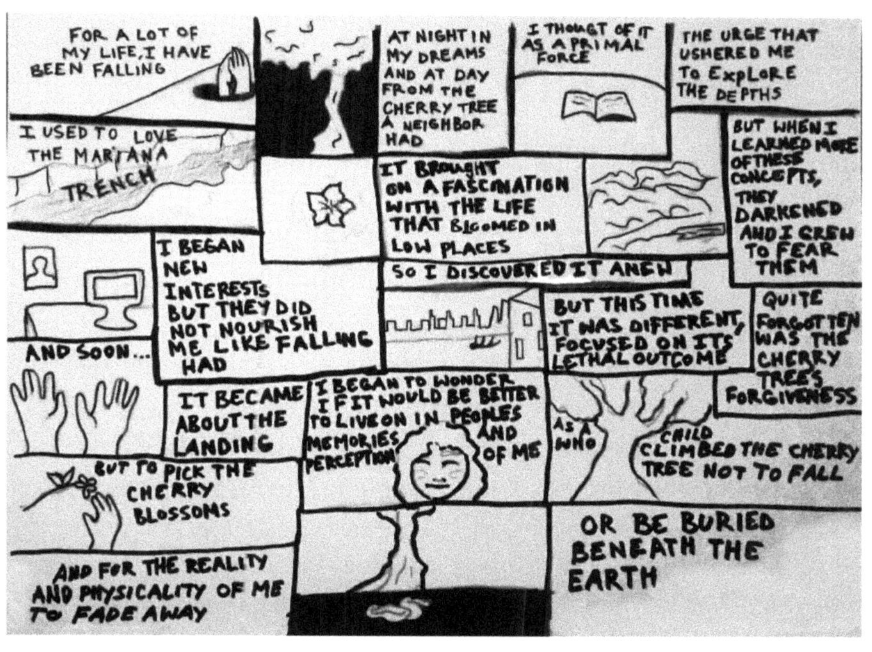

Frey Pokorny

Growing Things

In an empty subway station, grass and flowering weeds fight through cracked concrete and ivy vines twine around integral pillars and hanging, single-bulb lights. Trash and crumpled receipts shift and whisper across the floor, barely fluttering in the faint echo of a breeze which, at one point, might have had a life on the surface.

It does not belong to the surface anymore, of course. Those who come below rarely leave, and its dying breath will be only another routine intake of air in the lungs of one who does not understand the weight they carry.

A girl and a man sit on a bench. They are each in the possession of an unremarkable backpack. The girl slumps forward on the bench, her load secured on her shoulders. Her brow is set with the grim determination of one who shoulders her burden always because she must-- though that is less by choice, and more by necessity. She has not yet found a stop where it is safe to release the contents. The man, at least thirty years her elder, leans back against the bench. His pack sits by his feet, balanced gently against his leg like an obedient dog.

They are waiting for the train. They've been waiting for a long, long time. They might yet wait a while longer. At this station, all the schedules say "ARRIVING" "ARRIVING" "ARRIVING" without a trace of date or time or soon. At this station, the train comes for you.

It is kind of like tomorrow, in that regard.

The girl's eyes keep darting to the bag. Not hers, of course; she knows all too well its contents. She is rarely without their weight, but she is curious, oh so curious, about the man. Is his bag heavy? It does not look full, but then again, fears come in many shapes and sizes.

Can he tell, from looking, how many fears reside in hers?

The breeze dances around them, and the girl wonders what it might say if it could speak. Would it tease and taunt, mocking their prisons of physicality? Would it scoff at the weight of the feet which bind them to this concrete floor, and the weights they add to ensure that they will never know what it is like to soar?

Would it laugh? Drunk and giddy on the haughtiness its freedoms have grown and nursed into strength?

She wonders, and the breeze tugs at her hair, the loose wisps which will never stay down, no matter how she tries, and a new image blossoms like fireworks in the cinema behind her eyes.

Maybe it is just a wanderer. A traveler, a roamer, fragmenting into a million pieces every second and refusing to let that stand in its way. It does not always know where it is, or where it is going, or how it will be carried there, or who might split it along the way, but it does not stop.

It has been in symphonies. It has been caught, trapped, bottled, only to rocket from its prison every time. It has burned (oh, how many times it has burned). And it has brushed by a wilting houseplant, and the two have clasped hands in the briefest of silent solidarities before parting, both renewed.

There is no true way to tell, but- she thinks- she *wants* to believe that it is just as lost as she is.

A war of impulses stage on the battleground of her heart, and she is torn, suddenly and unexpectedly, by the urgent need to hold her breath against the breeze. To close her eyes and telepathically convey that *she does not want to be another careless neighbor, hurting it by all the ways she does not understand.*

Torn between that and the selfish want, desire, *lust* to breathe in deep and fill her lungs. To give it her story to tell too, because what if this train never comes? What if she herself goes grey on this bench, and this breeze is her last taste of the aboveground?

So maybe- maybe she will keep it with her. Like star crossed lovers, they will do the impossible. She will hold the breeze in her breath, and it will teach her to fly, and she will teach it the security of a wall to press against and be held by; the cold of bench against denim against skin, reminding one that *she. is. alive.*

The weight on her back groans with her secret fear, tucked away in secret pockets, ever swelling to accommodate *that she will never truly live.*

Her eyes skate again to the man, and his bag on the floor, and the peaceful droop of his eyelids as his thumbs whisper a gentle rhythm as they pass each other. She asked him once-- he calls it twiddling.

She waits.

She weighs.

She speaks.

"What's in yours?"

Her throat is dry, and the words are rough, made of sawdust and sandpaper and the staleness of the air here underground.

He takes a moment, but when he responds, his words sound as heavy as her bag.

"Would you like to see?"

She nods, even as the side pocket, the one farthest from him, the one he cannot see, inflates with *no.*

He reaches down, slow and deliberate. Of course it is deliberate. One does not bare their fears without deliberation.

He tugs the zipper on its track along the length of the bag, and pulls it open wide. The girl flinches, but nothing bursts except the orange flare of jealousy inside her heart. She can't even imagine opening the zipper of her bag more than the slightest of cracks, for fear that it might never shut again.

The man pulls a walking cane from the main pocket, folded neatly for convenient travel, and passes it to her. It is pretty, decorated with golden filigree; well-used, if not well loved.

"My father's father," he murmurs, tracing a finger over shimmering lines, "Was a hard man. He worked until the day he died, and expected everyone around him to do the same."

The cane is heavy and solid in her hands.

"My father," he continues, with a sigh that sounds like it might rip his frame in half, "Was a strong man. But his knee gave out when he was a few years younger than I am now. He could walk without a cane, but we all knew he needed it, and eventually he caved."

She passes it back, watches his grip grow tight around the handle before he snaps it back into its folded shape.

"His father nagged him every chance he got. Called him weak and frail, and joked about his old man bones. 'Look at me,' he'd say on more than one occasion, 'twice your age and twice as healthy too'. I was only a kid, but even I knew that if I turned out weak, there would be no sympathy from him."

"That's awful," the girl whispers, and the man smiles sadly.

"It is. It was a terrible way they learned to live, and I've been fighting tooth and nail so I do not repeat them."

He gazes at the cane, and there is no hatred in his eyes, only weariness.

"Ever since I crossed forty-five, I've been waiting. Will it be my back? My knee? One of those organs I can't live the same without?" A pause, a breath, a shudder rippling through the wryly spoken words. "My resolve, maybe. To be honest with you, I still haven't figured out exactly why it sticks with me. If I'm afraid of turning out like them or turning into them."

She is silent, and he hums, sliding the cane back into its place. It thumps against something, refuses to go all the way down, and he peers into the bag, chuckles, and reaches down to the bottom. "There's another one in here today."

Her heart stops, flutters, starts again, but he only pulls out a wallet, and she almost laughs through the relief that strangles her. Money. Fare, though this train rarely charges. It's common enough.

But the man does not stop. He leans back against the bench, flips the wallet open, and extends it to the girl.

She takes it. There is no money in this wallet. No cards which might decline, no identification with conflicting names, no appointment reminders or scribbled phone numbers. Instead, every pocket and flap and fold is stuffed with pictures, most of them of normal, harmless, friendly-looking people.

He sees her confusion; it is painted clearly across her face, and smiles. "Travelling companions."

"You're afraid of them?"

"Mmm." He smiles and holds out his hand. She hands him the wallet, but instead of tucking it back in the bag, he begins to pull the photos, one by one, from their slots.

"My best friends," he says softly. "My partner. Our daughter. My favorite teacher. The neighbor who took me in and gave me home cooked meals when classes got too much. There's nothing more terrifying than letting your starving heart be loved, and that's why they're the heaviest weight I carry."

"Oh," she says, and she might, she *might*, if she consults her eyes, be crying. "Oh."

He nods, and pats her gently, softly on the shoulder, just to the side of her backpack's straps.

After a moment more spent looking through the photos, he grunts, slipping the stack of photos in the breast pocket of his shirt and settling back on the bench.

"That's why I've learned that some things, you've gotta hold here," he taps his chest. "Right next to your heart. Not here," he taps her shoulder. "Because they wouldn't want you to. Because they love you, and sometimes you've got to learn to accept the love that other people are willing to freely give, even if you're still learning to believe that you don't need to deserve it. Balances you out better, that way."

She smiles, and it is tremulous and shaky like an earthquake, like the earth, like the ground around her is shaking, and the ground around her *is* shaking because the train, the train has finally come.

The man looks at her, and she looks anywhere but him. "Stay a minute. The train's coming for you; it'll wait. What's the biggest one in there?"

Her breath, already thick as gel, hitches, and he holds up a hand.

"You don't have to say it. Just picture it. Close your eyes, hold out your hands."

The train has brought more than just a breeze with it; it has brought entire winds. They swoop around her and she knows what she is afraid of more than anything.

"I'm assuming you've got it," he grunts, and there is a soft scraping and shuffling and something light and soft settles in her hands. Her eyes flicker open.

In her cupped hands, he has placed a dandelion. Soil still clings in clumps to the root, hardy and thick enough to push its way through concrete, small enough that the delicate offshoots tremble in her hands as the first cars of the train rush by.

"That's your fear." He says gently, and indeed her backpack does feel lighter. "Now put it in your pocket."

She does, feeling the cool moisture of the soil at her side.

"It's not everything, of course. Just a start; just so you don't forget."

She doesn't want to forget, but she isn't sure she trusts herself to remember.

"And it'll end up in your backpack anyway," the man keeps talking, raising his voice to be heard above the noise. "But you've got to keep putting it back. Always, always putting it back and eventually it'll root there."

"Okay," she whispers, even though the thought of standing, shouldering her bag without the support of the bench behind her makes her want to crumple and the sound of the screeching wheels pours through her ears and the mesh side pockets of her bag like infinite sand, "Okay."

"Good." The man smiles, pats her shoulder one last time, and nods. "I believe that one's for you."

"What about you?" She asks, and he smiles.

"I'm waiting for someone else. I'll catch the next one. Don't forget, you hear?"

She nods.

"Keep putting it back."

She nods again.

"Good. There you go."

The man leans back and closes his eyes, and she stands, planting her feet against the weight which feels just a little less like it will topple her this time. The train screeches to a stop, and the doors open with a puff of scented air, and she almost laughs out loud or maybe cries because the whole car is full of wildflowers.

And as a florist shuffles to the side and mumbles something sheepishly about deliveries,

and petals crease beneath her feet,

and her fingers rub against

the green and gold and growing thing

in the jacket pocket at her side,

as goldenrod and crocus

cherry blossoms; celandine

whisper soft against her cheek

she realizes that today

right now

she is not quite so afraid of living.

SJ Blasko

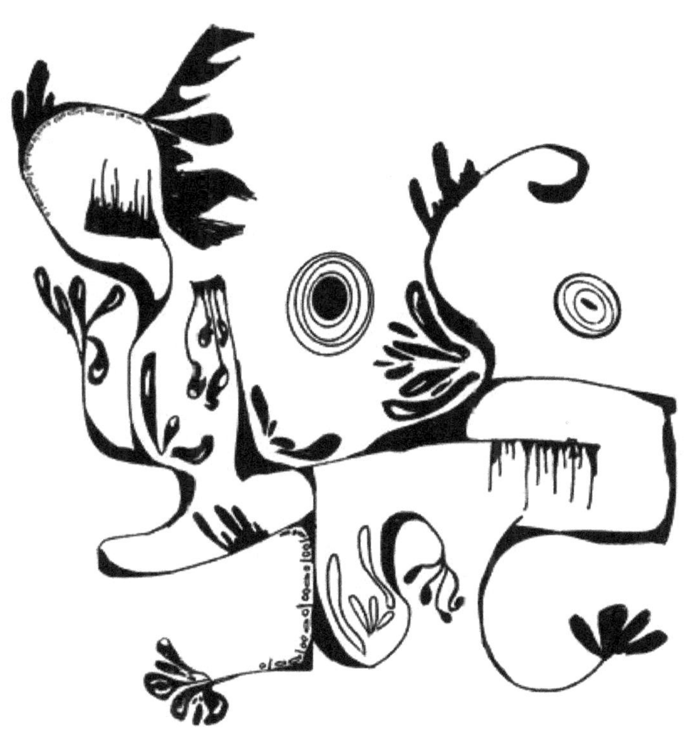

Erelah Emerson

The wind grazes, like a field of flocking sheep.
It caresses my cheekbones, with the softness of rose petals.
The sun fills my being with warmth, and it spreads to my
cheeks, that part into a smile.
Nearby a swallow twits and flitters,
And all the woodland creatures chime in with orchestrate
    harmony.
A symphony for the lonely, the wanderer, and the children
born of the moon.
Dog days of hot pavement and sticky arms come and go, but
the wind still tells me secrets.
The nightbirds sing their lullabies at dusk, and whistle into
the night as the sun dips below the jagged tree line made up
of all the trees I wished to climb when I was
    young.
Sometimes when it rains while the sun is out, I long for older
days, when time had less of an importance. When the date
wasn't as significant. When counting the hours wasn't
dreaded, but anticipated, so we could go out and
    play.
The summer heat brings back droves of joy in waves of
    nostalgia.
But I long still for the day after.
I still wake up and open my window to listen to the wind's
secrets. To listen to the twitting flitting composers positioned
up in the trees.
But sometimes it's okay to get lost in the songs, and
    remember how you got here.

Clover Zicolella

FOR YOU//TO BE LOVED

Dandelion:

> *both a flower and a weed*
> *simple joys, your inner child*
> *healing and survival,*

Juniper:

> *perfect loveliness*
> *beauty and*
> *protection*

Zinnia:

> *endurance, lasting friendship*
> *goodness and remembrance.*

Yarrow:

> *lasting love,*
> *healing, inspiration, joy.*
> *often given to show concern for one's well-being.*

a horoscope in flowers pt. x
goldenrod- december 21st to january 19th

capricorn
guarded and cautious
so afraid of what is inside you that you would rather
play sentinel to your own self
than let someone see how you are doing
you do not have to stand watch alone, capricorn
your hallowed halls empty and cobwebbed
ballrooms barren of people
in fear of what lies beneath your castle
ancient rules strict in their conduct
so no one has to see who you really are
but capricorn, your caution grows over you like weeds
obscuring the face of your stalwart nature
your dedication to those you love
a keystone, a foundational stone
supporting them with everything you have
the steadiness of your heart that you fear so much
breathe in, capricorn. breathe out. and let go.

Your lucky numbers are 48, 20, and 6.

Gaia

There came a day
Where a choice had to be made

The right way or the easy way

And you chose the right way

You say my name
And I see the blink
Of a hope made small reality

That you know
And love me
Not despite that
But because of it
I'll always owe you that

R. Sunshine

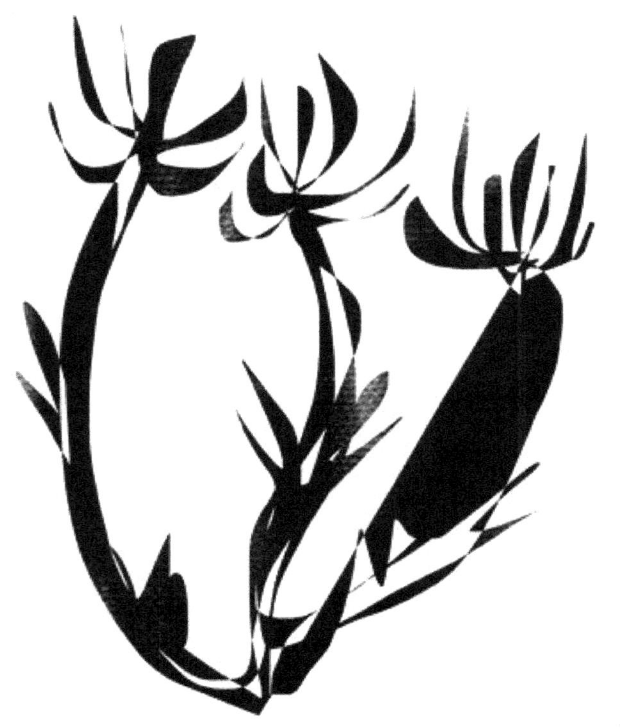

Erelah Emerson

the noose

you know the verses.
"don't be anxious.
cast your cares on Him."
but your mind is a jumble of
what ifs and perceived failures
that won't disappear
no matter how hard you beg them to.
impervious to logic
impossible to dislodge
like guests who have overstayed their welcome.

just pray, they say.
just talk to God
and everything will work itself out.
but you can't speak
through constricted lungs
can't squeak out a prayer
besides "help me."
sometimes He's
not even on your mind
when it's all you can do
to keep breathing
in
out
repeat.

and sometimes your prayers
fall on deaf ears

and your stomach keeps churning
and your heart is thump thump thumping
against your ribcage
and your skin buzzes with energy
that escapes through the
tap tap tapping of your limbs
and the noose around your neck
squeezes and squeezes
sinister and snakelike
invisible and insidious
and you're choking and gasping
for reasons they can't fathom.

Soon the floor will drop out beneath you
and the stress will snap your neck
crack like a bullet
but for now you gasp for air
caught in the harshness
between living and dying.

they don't understand.
they look at you
and see failure,
spiritual and mental,
as if you don't already hate yourself enough
for your shortcomings.
they berate you for crying
for not holding it together
for not trusting God enough.

it's just you and God versus the noose

but sometimes it feels like it's just you.
sometimes it feels like you've failed too many times
at pushing away the noose
and God has given up on you,
is ashamed to call you His child.
shame that weighs on you
and drags you into self-loathing.

why can't you just trust God more?
why does this noose hover
ever-present around your neck
waiting to conflate something small
into an impassible obstacle?
why can't this thorn in your flesh
leave you alone?

the tears worsen the noose.
the sobs catch in your throat
and you can't breathe
gasping, silently screaming,
wishing for this cup to pass from you.

you're empty
hollowed out after the tears are spent
nothing but a frenetic mess.
not enough energy to love others
or yourself.

but in your emptiness
He finds you.
He lifts your chin

caresses your tear-stained cheeks
restores the breath to your aching lungs.

but I'm empty, you say.
I have nothing for You.

there was nothing you could give
that would earn My love, He says.
then He cries with you
knowing the emptiness
knowing the terror
knowing the judgment you face.
and when His tears are spent,
He fills you.

when the noose returns,
you still ache.
you still struggle for breath
struggle to keep your stomach's contents down
struggle to keep your raging thoughts at bay.
but you know He's there
right by your side
holding your broken form without judgment.
and He will fill you again
and again
and again
because that's what He does best—
He restores broken things.

Cassandra Hamm

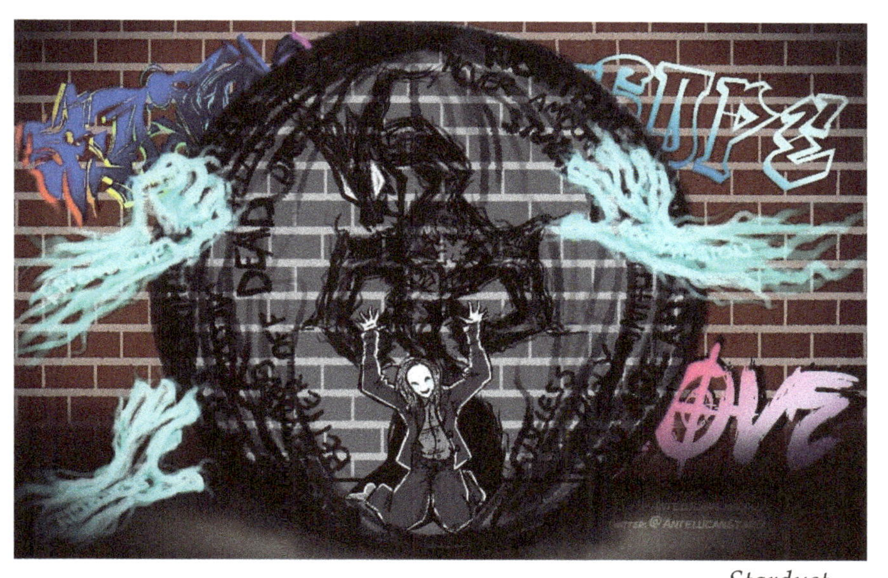

Stardust

you stand there, withered,
hoping someone would see you.
I found you, withered.

the sky clears, sun shines,
I stretch in your direction.
let me support you.

standing hand in hand,
we reach toward the bright sun
letting growth begin.

—let's be sunflowers together.

Kimmy Renee

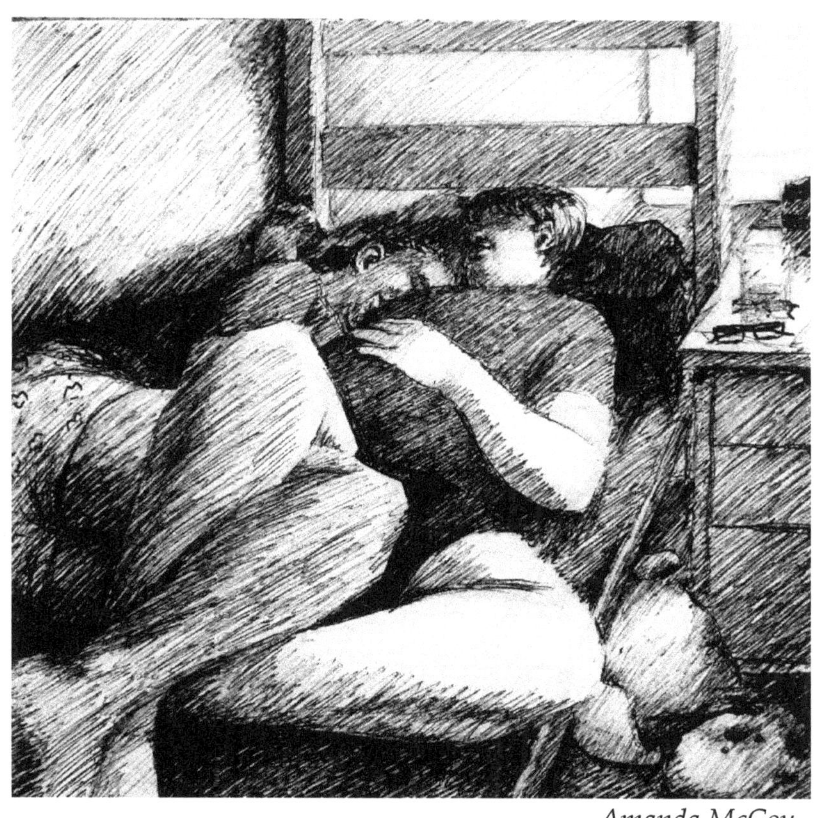

Amanda McCoy

quiet as a dew filled morning
when im crying
there you are

when i find myself ablaze
in quiet rage
there you are

when im sinking underground
lips wont move or make a sound
you pull me up with love abound
in silent hope
there you are

OJR

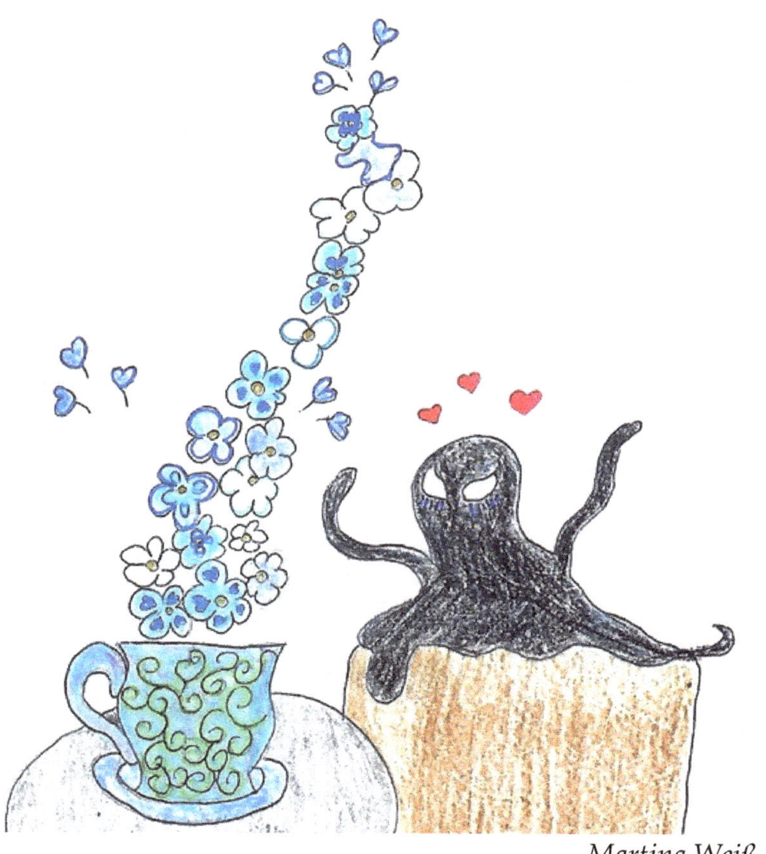

Martina Weiß

**(The lesser-known name for amaranth is just a bit more
    inclusive)**

In your garden, hand-picked pockets
Were happy singing you a song
But now the garden has been trampled,
(the flowers did no wrong,)
But do you blame them-
for their deadness,
Do you belittle their insides?

When it's not their fault their petals
Were plucked and left to dry.

You used to tell me your garden
(flourished,)
and I'm sure that once was true,
You held a celebration when the seedlings
showed their heads and called to you;
I cannot wonder what it must be like
To watch their leaves
All
Fall,
I have no garden,
I have no pockets,
So I'll wrap them in my shawl.

When you see my crochet tippet,
When there are no stems left around,
I cannot help you when you fall as well
And dig into the ground.

There are no seeds left,
I want to tell you,
They have been eaten by the birds-
But your garden was your livelihood,
You're dying with my words.

You tell me life is fatal,
You tell me clay pots are never glad,
I sweep
The leaves
Left in your wake; I ache when you are sad

You tell me you are scared,
You tell me you're afraid,
But I am no gardener,
There's nothing I can say,

You hand me a broken butterfly weed,
But I only shake my head, for I'm not walking away from
    you
When your grieving fills with dread-
The empty gardens,
can't you hear them?
The way their anger cries for glue,
I want to say
it's not your fault
that people trampled over you,

Flowers are a beauty in their gardens,
How their stretch marks are beloved,
But the petals of your fingers

Have been burned
And charred
And shoved,

I want to say
Not everyone will understand that this beauty is new,
I want to say that *being broken doesn't mean you're worthless,*
    too.

I want to say there is so much more to pockets in a pot

But you are tired of when the tourists
Destroy your foliage
Without a thought.

I walk you outside one morning, so you can feel the spread,
How your flowers are still dancing,
But they're dancing with the dead,

This two-step symphony of flowers
That you created with your teeth
Has been dismantled; but that doesn't mean You've
    forgotten how to breathe;

Your garden sits among the multitudes
Of new things it can now be,
And we will mourn the loss of what it was
And of what we cannot see-
You tell me you are afraid,
You tell me you are tired,
So I'll wrap my hands around your eyes,

(I don't call you a liar.)
I cannot understand what losing this
Must have meant to you,
But I know that it was special,
So I'll help you get this through.

I give you seedlings that are screaming out-
but I can never die,
I tell you it's okay to know that
Sometimes plants can lie,
This pink and fluffy, hanging cloud, that we fill your new
    garden with- still hums,

It's not immortal, despite what they say,
but we'll deal with that when it comes.

You can begin again
When you have fallen,
No matter what you want to allow;
And I will stand over the picket fence,
Even if I don't know how,

You tell me of always dying,
Of now
Being afraid to grow-
But there is an *us* in amaranth,
And you won't always be alone.

Erelah Emerson

My mother taught me patience when she taught me how to garden. We lived in an old apartment on Sterling street. I was seven. Confined to a small backyard with little room for such a creation, it was there where she taught me the diligence behind planting a seed and waiting for it to grow.

Now, enveloped in courage, I give seeds to every soul I cross paths with. I think of them as open ended blessings. I wonder how many people have planted those seeds or how many people have stuck around and watched a seed grow into fractions of hope. I wonder how many people gave up along the journey.

I remind myself that not everyone carries patience around like an old antique that gains value the older it gets.

When my mother taught me patience she was never direct in her message. Instead she just taught me how to garden and appreciate the abundance of vegetables that came as a result. I think it was because she wanted me to discover a sense of meaning in all of the small things by myself.

Now I am twenty-two years old and behind me is a never ending trail of flowers and plants and vegetables, some of which are in full bloom, some of which are not, but all of which are beautiful.

I thank my mother, a warrior and a teacher, who showed me how to grow in the first place.

Kath Kane

Lorna & Bryoni

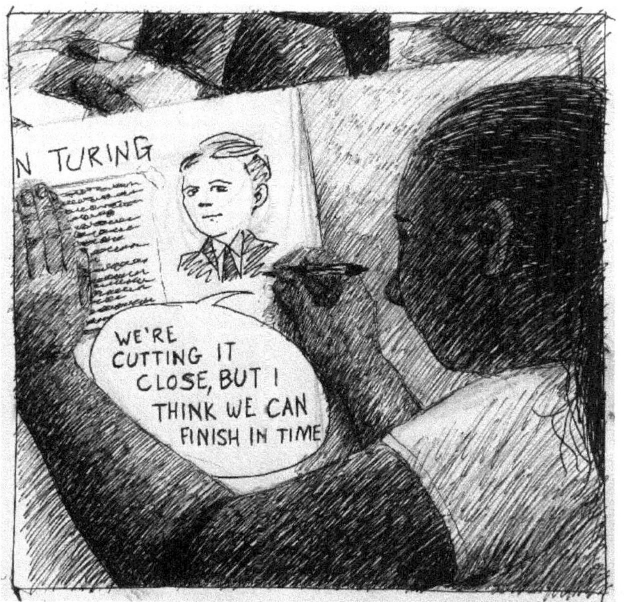

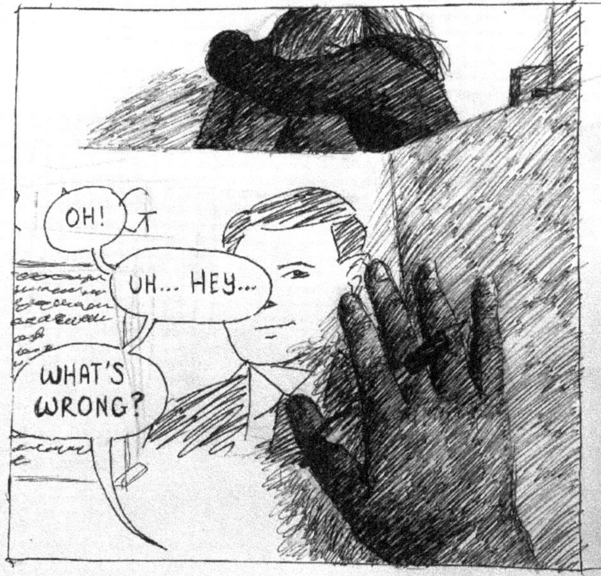

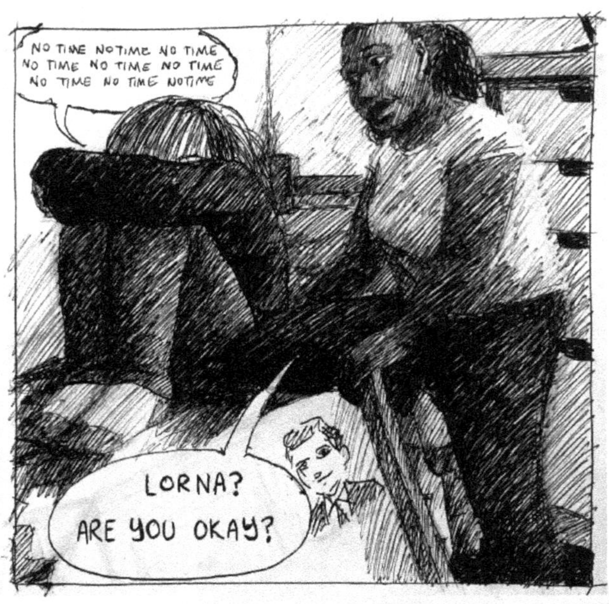

NO TIME NOTIME NO TIME NO TIME NO TIME NO TIME NO TIME NO TIME NOTIME
LORNA?
ARE YOU OKAY?

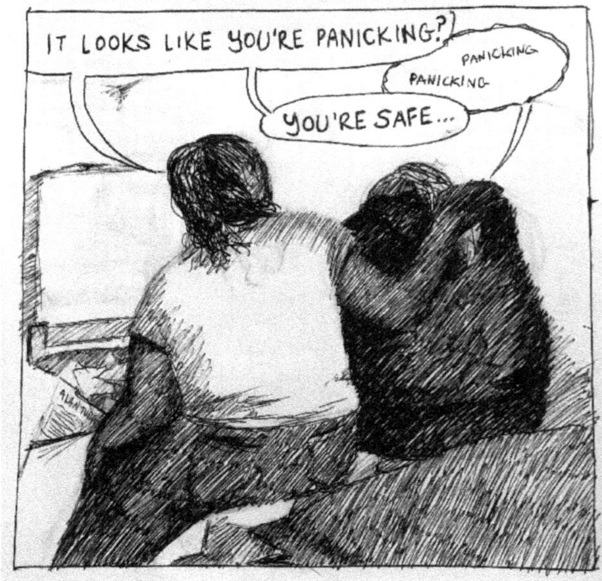

IT LOOKS LIKE YOU'RE PANICKING?
PANICKING PANICKING
YOU'RE SAFE...

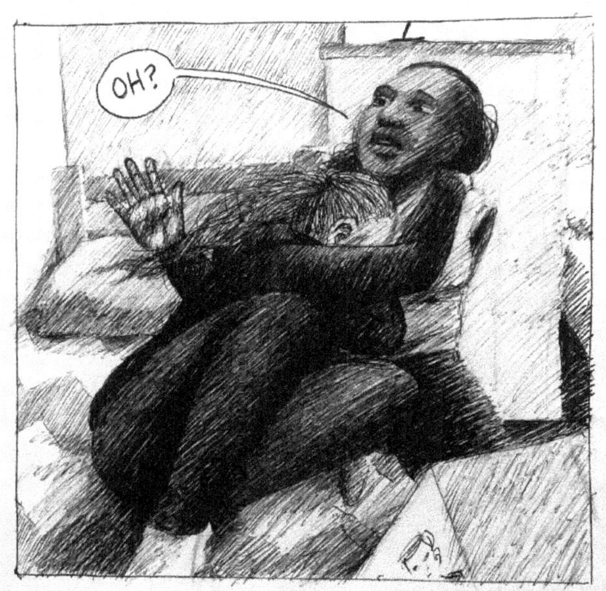

OH?

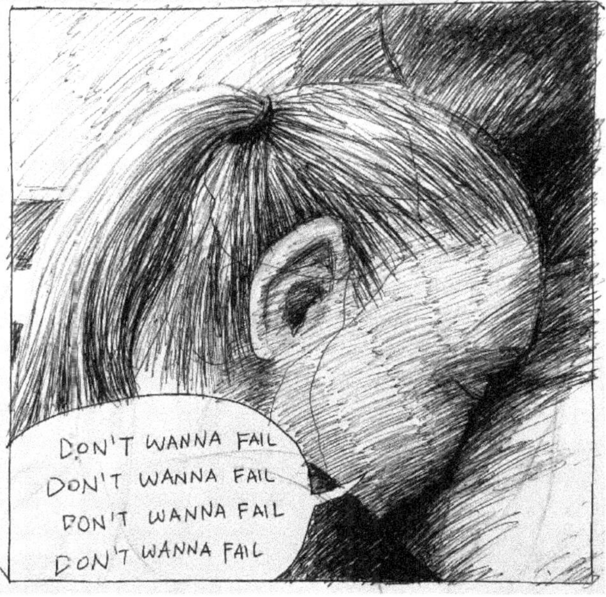

DON'T WANNA FAIL
DON'T WANNA FAIL
DON'T WANNA FAIL
DON'T WANNA FAIL

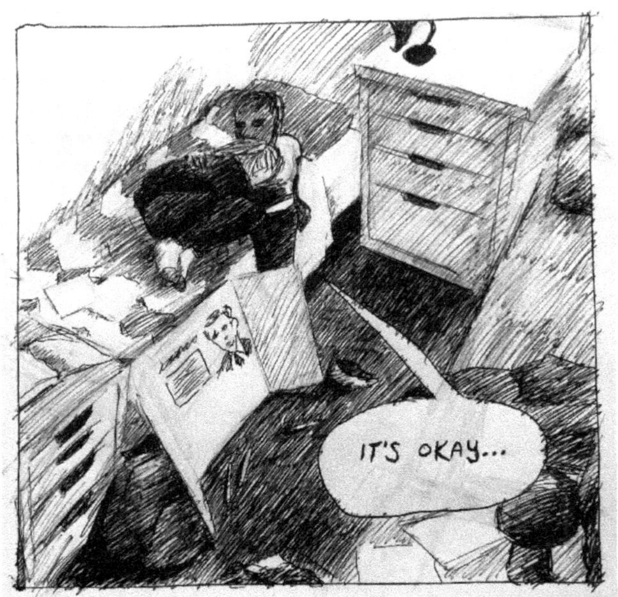

Find more Lorna and Bryoni on Instagram: @lornaandbryoni

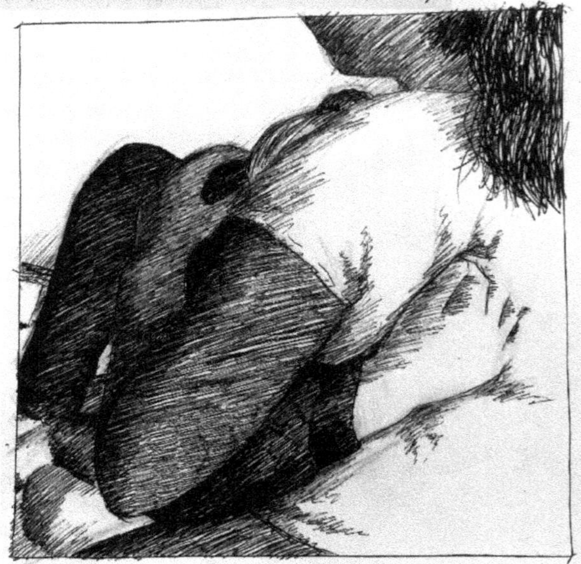

Amanda McCoy

Celandine tea

The closest thing to a soulmate
I'll ever have
Is that something close to a sunflower,
That something close to hands,
The closest thing
To happy, that I've ever felt, at all,
Was picking Celandine
And mixing it
With hot water and thyme;
My garden is not full of Kings
That grow veins with such worth,
But full of weeds and dandy
And spice that burns
The earth,
The closest thing to yellow, burns,
As I chug it down,
I wish the petals
Could burst with light,
But in Celandine
I drown;
My teacup steams with worry,
The smoke says
-There are joys to come-
That I should drop the tea
And crumble,
Maybe find some cherry gum,
The closest thing to a soulmate

That I'll ever have,
Is the wilting, yellow flowers that
Remind me of the sun.

Erelah Emerson

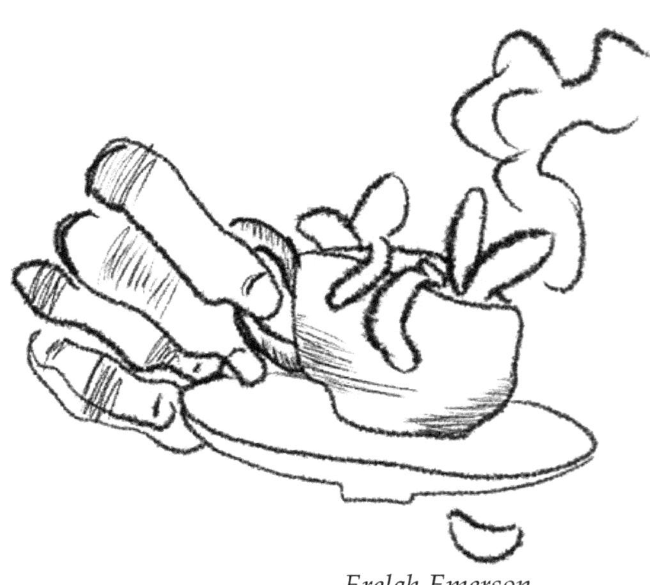

Erelah Emerson

Do Not Worry

Do not worry
About the size of your life or the shape of your body
or the sound of your voice, just sing
loudly
or soft, if you prefer
Do not worry
In this world, if you will be known or terribly clever
or rich, even, for if your belly is filled and you have one
    friend
or two
you are there
Do not be concerned
With whether you will find love or not
(but if you are in love, be so in love as to be reckless)
love will find you
instead…
go out to the sea or up to the mountains
or into the woods, running, of course
sleep out underneath that expanse, which is night
which is everything

Theo Oliver

Erelah Emerson

FOR A HOME//TO STAY

Wildflower:

a flower of an uncultivated variety
a flower growing freely

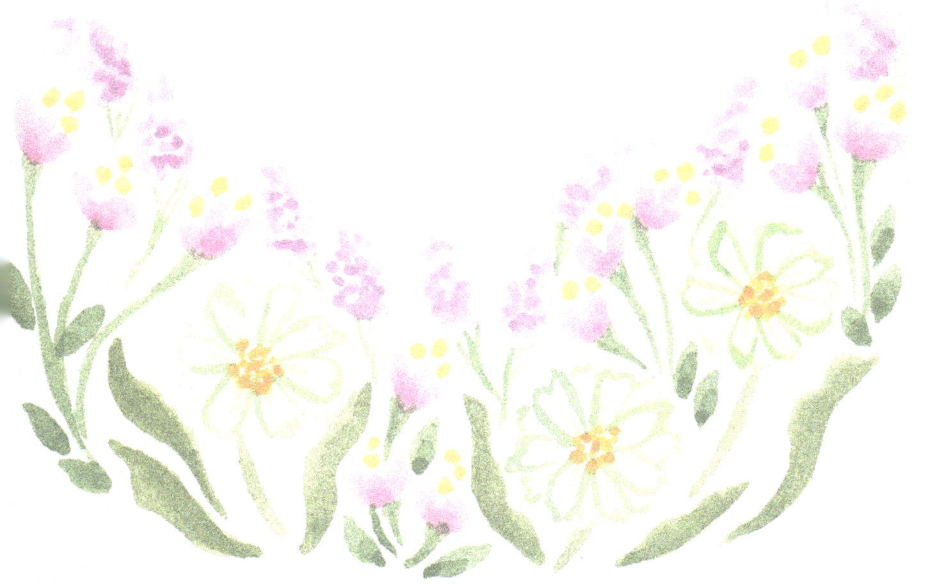

a horoscope in flowers pt. xi
cherry blossom- january 21st to february 20th

flights of fancy are
what you are used to, aquarius
used to running as far as the muscles in your legs would
    allow you
best not to think or dwell on unfortunate things
but aquarius, you cannot run forever
and in the dark of the night
the cool of a shadow
you deserve to feel rested and not haunted
tortured by missed moments and
the absence of a nest
if you can manage to stop
(a terrible burden, one not to be taken on lightly but)
i think you will find a home there
a place to be warm and loved and free
in a way that running will not give you

Your lucky numbers are 1, 53, and 74.

Mundane

You have your place
Among the ever so mundane,
Yet miraculous pleasures
Brought forth by this life;
Yellow tips to leaves come the heat of summer
Bitter, prestorm air, splitting every hair
Wilted dandelions left to rot on the fresh lawns
Fallen eggshells
And their once homely nests.

You have your place
Among the routine silver linings;
The accidental clovers, littered in patches
Distant fireworks, hopeful fun
Sunburn before the pain
Confidential whisperings, secret trusts
Closed bedroom doors.

You are the painful upbringings
And the forgotten memories
Dancing alone, pressing your feet into
Broken glasses
The romanticized flowers
Filling the blissful summer void.

You are the empty gardens
Dried out soil,

Rotting bugs
Cast aside, painting your walls
Lay the marigolds meant to coat your mind,
Not a single petal making its way through.

Riley Marie Courtney

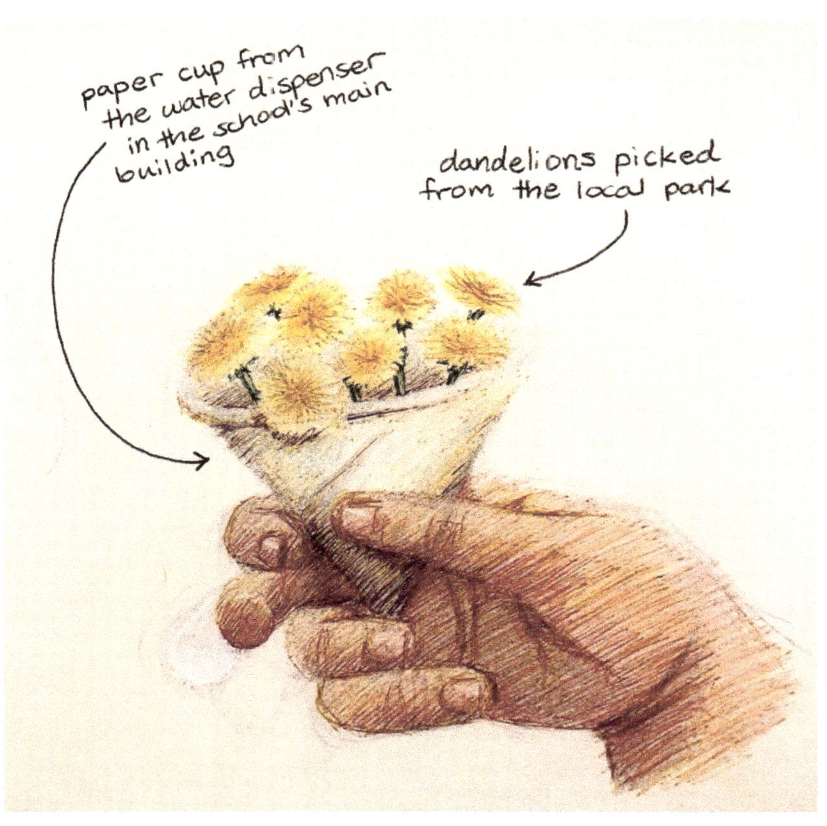

Amanda McCoy

Dandelion Whispers

oh, to whisper to the dandelions, telling them the secrets that
fill our minds. we find ourselves giddy to find a full, fluffy
cloud that's ready to hear our wishes.
with our eyes closed, a soft breath, a quiet mutter then blow.
now, the wish goes throughout the universe to be fulfilled.
dandelions whisper amongst themselves, the wind swaying
them as if they're dancing. the sun beams, the warmth
hugging us while our wishes are heard—
dandelion whispers are louder.
we
are
heard.
nature surrounds us, bringing us back from the darkest
times. from the dandelions, to the sun, to the wind— we are
all embraced and welcomed. and sometimes, that's just the
wish we need.

Kimmy Renee

CICADAS AND COFFEE AND ROSES

My husband wakes up for work at 5:30am. I am sitting on the couch, watching the news. He already knows what my answer will be, but he asks anyway. "Have you slept at all?" I shrug. He knows I haven't slept. He knows I haven't slept in days. He is stoic, but I know if I look up from the television, I will see his expression. It will be a little sad. It will be a little frightened. I can't stand the thought that I have done this to him. He sighs and walks away. I assume it is to gather his thoughts and begin again. He makes us each a cup of coffee, mine in my favorite heart shaped mug. He uses the fancy, flavored creamer. He knows exactly how I take my coffee on mornings like this. After so many years of mornings like this, he knows too many things. His kindness breaks my heart.

He sits across from me and mutes CNN. He begins to gently pour his words on me like round fat warm summer rain, each drop pregnant with the possibility of growth. I know he is praying that something he says will land on fertile ground. Grow something stronger and more resilient.

He says, "This is what it feels like to live an ordinary life."

He says, "This is what it feels like to sleep in the dip in the mattress, worn soft in the middle after years of dreaming, belly to back."

He says, "This is the way people drink their coffee."

He says, "This is the way people grow old."

I can barely hear him over the din of sounds inside my noisy head. This is the way mania affects me. It makes me feel like my head is bursting at the seams, cracking open like a cicada shell. Like a cicada who has slept for seventeen years and whose wings are finally free to rip open the dark. When I am like this, I want to start fires. I want to plant roses at midnight. I want to gamble away our savings. I want to wager on horses and new dresses. Impulsivity nips at my heels.

He says, "Take your pills, Honey, and try to remember what it feels like to sleep through the night.

He says, "Be still and this will pass."

"I don't know if I want it to pass this time." I say quietly. It has been long enough since my last manic episode that I have almost forgotten the unspeakable pain and shame that follows. Almost forgotten, but not completely. I know with certainty that I have said these words before. Still, he listens patiently, nodding to indicate he is taking it all in. I know he will never understand just how dark the darkness can be, or the way it feels taking the first few steps into mania. It feels almost euphoric. Euphoric, until the madness sets in.

Sunrise, sunset. Sunrise, sunset. We go around like this for a few days, then I relent and call my psychiatrist. I pretend that I am angry, but really, I am so very relieved. My doctor is responsive. He listens to the calm way I say, "I'm not feeling well." He listens but he also watches my knee shake, watches my hands flutter across my lap like little birds. He decides it is time to update my medication cocktail. Add a new mood stabilizer. We choose together, the one with the least possible side effects. I am ready. I crave sleep like a lost lover.

After so many years of doing this, I know that calm will find me. I understand that I will sleep and wake to a different view of the world. I understand that I have an illness and need medication. Still, there is a very fundamental part of me that harbors the shame of hurting the people that love me most. I am devastated at the idea that I have sent my husband off to work with the image of me - hair wild, eyes wilder, drinking coffee, glued to the worst news of the day. How do I reconcile my desire to be well with my willingness to slip back into the old patterns? Shame can be as bitter as any pill prescribed to heal. Shame, and the ugly things we tell ourselves to feed that shame. I will have to remember to talk with my therapist about this. I will have to write down what I am feeling and thinking today, so that when the memory of this fades, my treatment can still be effective. I have begun to keep notes for her, so that I can tell her each important event, before the medicine sooths the hurts and I forget again, about the cicada and the coffee and the roses.

Suzanne Lea

A thing which does not fade

In the morning, I get up
I wander through your quiet house
I catch my breath and root it deeply in my lungs
I breathe.
In the morning,
I weave queen anne's lace into my hair
And pretend it has not wilted overnight
Everything wilts, but sometimes
All it needs is water to come back.
When i was little,
I used to keep flowers
Sticks and leaves
Tucked away in corners of my room
Until they crumbled or molded or rot
/Often I still do/
But more and more, I'm learning to let go
To thank them, and return them to the earth
To blow a kiss and let the new things grow
In the morning
And the noontime and the evening
And the hours I never stay awake long enough to see on my
    own
Your home is my escape, a sanctuary
And on this morning it does not banish the darkness, not all
    the way
But that's okay because it's honest
I did not learn to build a mask within these walls

And you, *you* have always been my safety
Which does not change
As you stroke my heavy head
Understand me when the silence steals my tongue
And hold me, shaking limbs and all, throughout the night
you remind me i am not alone

Tonight i will be home
In a place familiar from a hundred dreams ago
But entirely too far away
From you, and from the version of this girl
Who threads her hair with queen anne's lace
Who scrubs at grime and takes up space—
Maybe that is why i cling
To a flower you picked
And carried in gentle hands to me
for me

Even still
I am learning to let go of the impermanent
To free my hands for clinging tighter
To the things which do not fade

-and love i love the way
     you make me believe i can be one of them

SJ Blasko

(The fleeting nature of life)

You will not be around for long,
she said,
In the blush of something cute
we are both just falling cherry blossoms
in a steep downward pursuit

(You will not be around for long,
she whispered,
tilting branches to the sky,
so there's no reason to leave me quicker,
even if you don't see why.)

Erelah Emerson

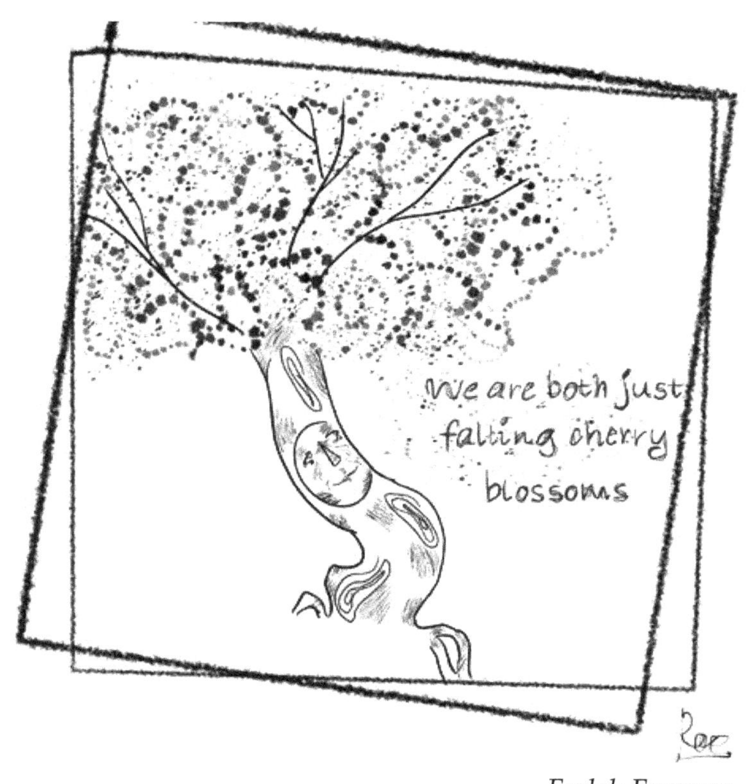

Erelah Emerson

a horoscope in flowers pt. xii
verbena- february 19th to march 20th

gentle pisces
your sunshine smile and your flower hands
are something you give freely
even though some have burnt you before, you still persist
you are lovely in your kindness
saintlike in your generosity
but remember that you too deserve the softness you give
    others
that you are allowed to breathe
to be angry, to be frustrated
to heal, and to grow
but growing in a garden means that sometimes you take up
    the space of others
that sometimes you must stand up for yourself
you should not have to boil alone
fear and anger simmering in the same pot
look around, pisces
you are in a garden
let yourself grow alongside others
and you will be happier for it

Your lucky numbers are 28, 42, and 39.

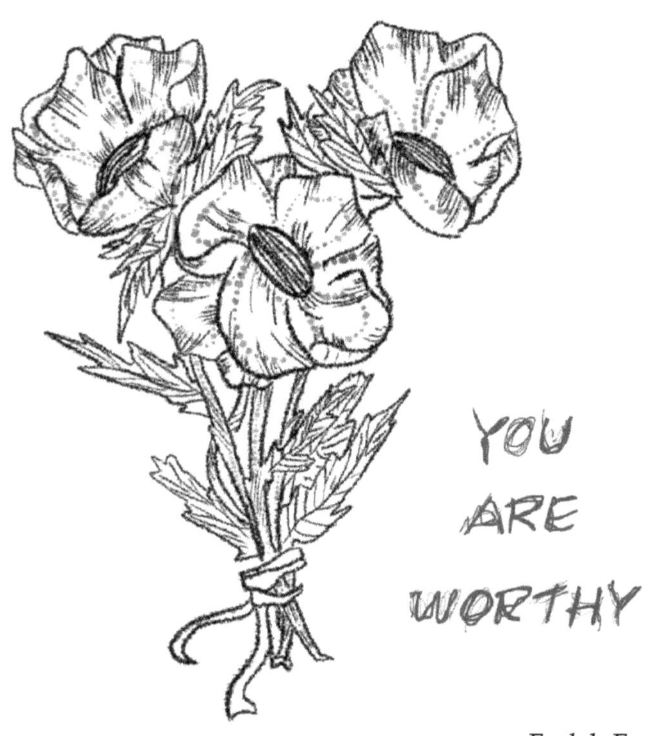

Erelah Emerson

AUTHOR BIOS

Bios marked with an asterisk are returning contributors from There Is Us

Becky B.* is a Canadian writer. While writing has been a lifelong passion of hers, she's only recently decided to share her words with the world. Previously published in the There is Us anthology, Becky is thrilled to be once again included with a group of such talented artists.

You can find more of her work on Instagram at @whimsical_jottings.

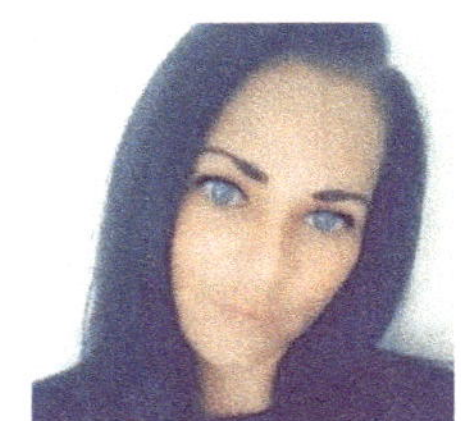

Sarah Birch of Studio 13 is a self-taught artist, who has been creating art professionally since 2018. She is currently based in the South West of the UK and specializes in fine art using graphite and charcoal to create realism and is well known for capturing the inner essence of her subject(s). Sarah currently has works exhibited in galleries in the South West, UK and also showcases her commissioned pieces on her social media.

You can find Sarah on Facebook: @studio13.artist, or on Instagram: @studio_13_artist

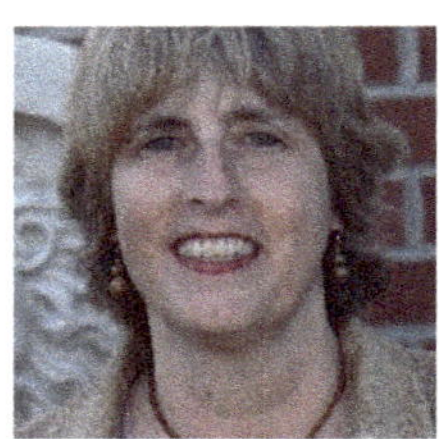

Maggie D. Brace is a long-time denizen of Maryland, teacher, gardener, basketball player and author. She attended St. Mary's College of Maryland and Loyola University, Maryland. She has written *'Tis Himself: The Tale of Finn MacCool* and *Grammy's Glasses*, and has both tied with Anne Tyler in the Baltimore Sun Paper Reader's Choice for best local writer as well as lost out to John Waters. As heady as this sounds, she remains a humble scrivener and avid reader presently aging gracefully in situ.

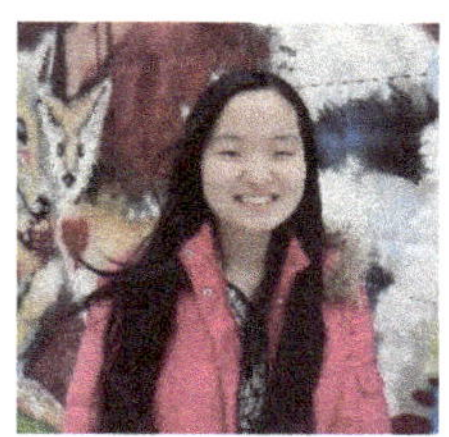

Maggie Chang is a poet, writer and photographer based in Toronto, currently completing her Bachelor of Environmental Studies. Having loved reading all her life, she started writing fiction when she was twelve, and she branched out to poetry, primarily spoken word, as a teen. At the same time, wanting to capture the beauty in the world led to an interest in photography. Her work focuses on environmentalism, intersectional feminism, and identity – particularly the joys and sorrows of being Chinese-Canadian. She has performed at Stories of Ours, and Living Hyphen's Birthday, her work has also appeared in Cultural Weekly, The Herd Archive, and Held Magazine.

You can find Maggie's work on Instagram: @seethewaymaggiecees

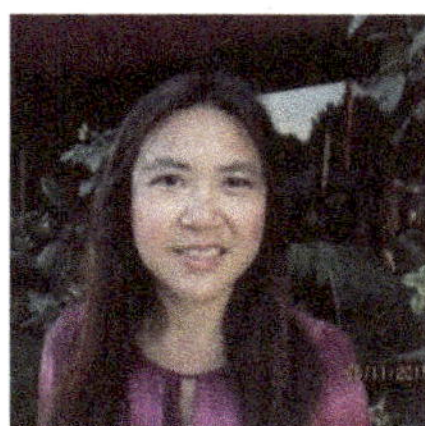

Jackie Chou is a neurodivergent poet residing in sunny Southern California who writes free verses and short form poetry. Her work has been published in Poetry Super Highway, Lummox, Altadena Literary Review, Dreamwell One Hundred Memories Anthology, and others.

Riley Courtney is a teenage author from Cincinnati, Ohio. She started writing in the first grade and has been writing ever since, though in the past couple years it has begun to play a larger role in her life. She dreams of being an author and turning her passion into a career. As an introvert, writing has become her form of communication and interaction with the world around her. You will never see her without a notebook or her laptop, and she almost always has a book with her. She is currently working on a YA Dystopian series and has recently published her debut poetry collection, Ode to Persephone.

You can find Riley on Instagram: @unopenedjournal

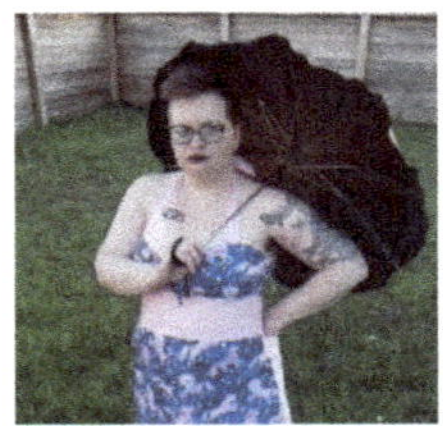

Jessica Critcher is a writer and textile artist currently living in Alameda, California. She has a degree in English from the University of Hawaii. Her work, both written and stitched, centers on questions about gender and mortality. She takes a particular interest in juxtaposing seemingly contradictory ideas: the cute and the macabre, rage and hope.

When she's not hidden behind her computer or sewing machine, you can find her baking scones, playing videogames, or throwing axes.

Follow her on Instagram @Crafting4Justice or @JessCritcher to learn more about her work, and to be bombarded with pictures of her spoiled chihuahua, Ada Lovelace.

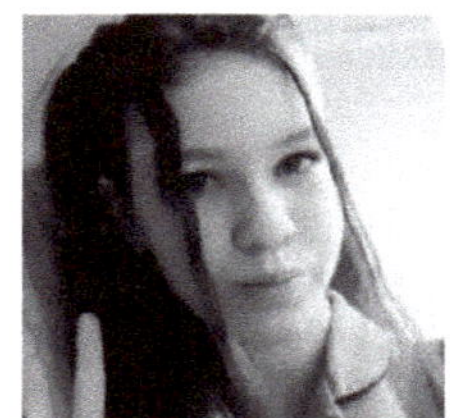

Lucinda Cylights* is a fourteen year-old girl from Australia. She spends most of her time reading, writing, and taking photos. Working on this anthology has been a highlight of 2020, and she hopes you thoroughly enjoyed it.

You can find more about her writing on Instagram @Queenie_the_writer_10 and you can find her photography on Instagram @wolf_cub_photography10

Rae (Erelah Emerson)* is simply a person that exists sometimes. They like to haphazardly draw characters from other people's novels, hang out with their lizard, and watch tv on mute even when people get mad about it. They have written and self-published one poetry book titled *Erratic and Unnecessary*, and they are hoping to write more books in the future. This is their second time being published with other authors.

You can find Rae on Instagram @poetry.rae or @bro.etry

Ojo Olumide Emmanuel is a poet and book editor. His works have appeared and are forthcoming at Feral, Quills, Poets in Nigeria (PIN), African Writers Space (WSA), The Nigerian Review (TRN) and elsewhere.
He is a fellow of SprinNG Writers Fellowship.

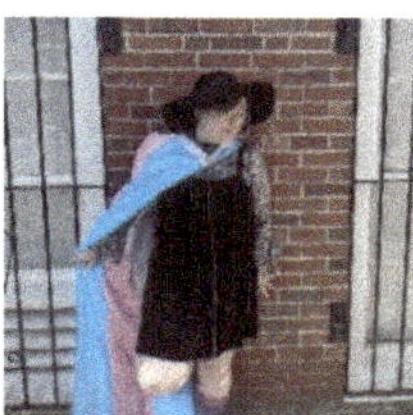

Adrien Farinas* is the person your parents warned you about, you know, that one. Allegedly born in Pottstown, Pennsylvania, xe has decided to inflict xir poetry on the public in a move that some call "daring", "bold", and "please get that microphone out of my face why are you asking me this". Xe enjoys short walks on the beach, sunsets, and long rants about obscure topics.
You can find more of xir poetry on goldenlightofthedawn.tumblr.com

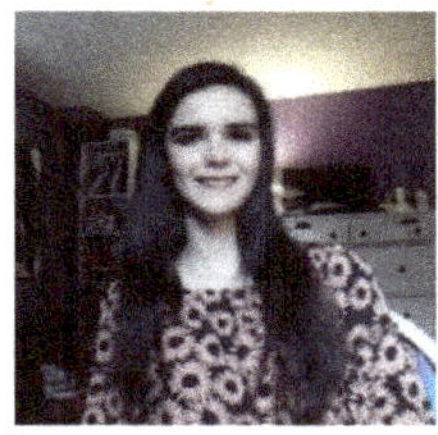

Margaret Ferreira* is a nineteen year-old student at Framingham State University. Their major is in English and they plan on using an English degree to pursue a career in teaching. In their free time, Margaret writes poetry and prose. Alongside a career in teaching, they hope to have a career in creative writing as well. Margaret became a member of their university's art and literary magazine, The Onyx, in the fall of 2019 and attends open mic nights on campus. Utilizing opportunities at Framingham State University has given Margaret the confidence to share their work outside of open mic nights.

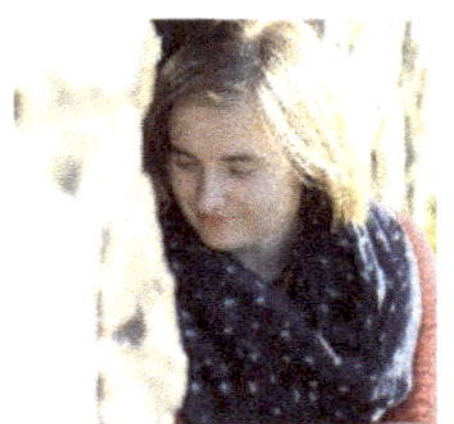

Beka Gremikova is an author, artist, and woman of faith who lives and dreams from the Ottawa Valley, Ontario, Canada. Her passions include travelling, folklore and myth, and nerding out over anime, manga, and *The Legend of Zelda*. Her previous publications include short stories in the *A Kind of Death* anthology from Uncommon Universes Press, the *Bingeworthy* anthology from Havok Publishing, and multiple flash fiction pieces on the Go Havok website. She's struggled with both anxiety and depression for the past number of years and hopes to help raise awareness of mental health struggles, especially within the Church. *You can find her on Twitter @DreamofWriting, Facebook, and Instagram.*

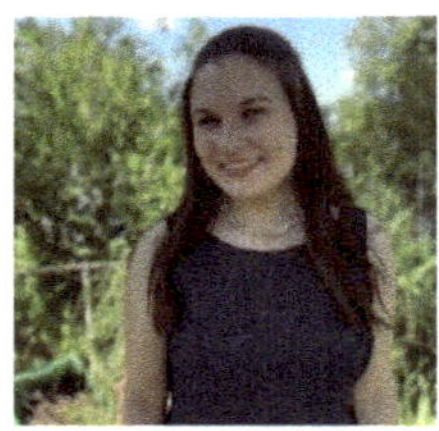

Cassandra Hamm has always been fascinated by the inner workings of the human mind. She received her B.S. in psychology and continues to apply her knowledge to her characters. Her stories have been published with Havok Publishing, Spark Flash Fiction, and Story Embers and have been included in multiple anthologies. Her passion for mental health, fueled by her own struggles with generalized anxiety disorder, often bleeds its way into her stories. She hopes that others will find hope amidst the anguish of inward struggles.

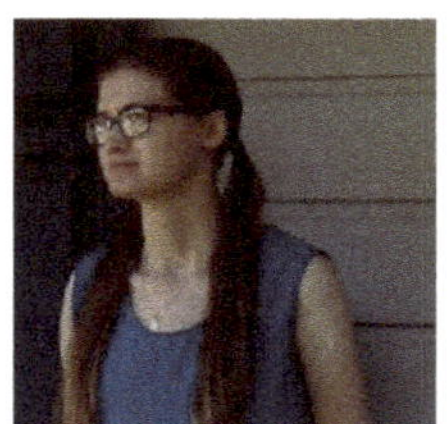

Katie Hanna is a die-hard Hufflepunk who writes stories about hopeful people in hard situations. She's passionate about history, fantasy, folklore, and contemporary social issues, and she's quite capable of mixing all of the above. Be warned.

You can learn more about Katie, her projects, and her obsession with Maggie Stiefvater at iamcharlesbakerharris.wordpress.com

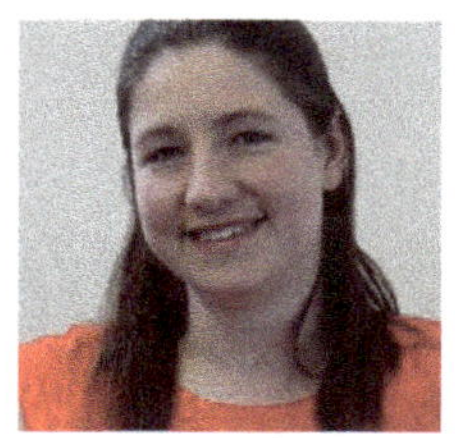

Sarah Hindmarsh is a private tutor and writer from England. She is the author of the ever popular "1001 Writing Prompts" series and the award-winning "Animal Adventures" series for 5 to 8 year-olds. She also has a growing number of short stories and poems published in various literary journals, magazines and anthologies. Sarah is currently working on her first fantasy novel.

The "Faces to the Sun" anthology is particularly important to her due to her own struggles with depression and anxiety, which started at a young age as the result of growing up gay and autistic in a world that, at the time, was not very tolerant of those things. When not writing or teaching Sarah can usually be found at the stables training her horses, Havana and Callie, or walking her miniature poodle, Kohla.

Follow Sarah on twitter @creating_Kohla or find her on Facebook @sarahhindmarshauthor

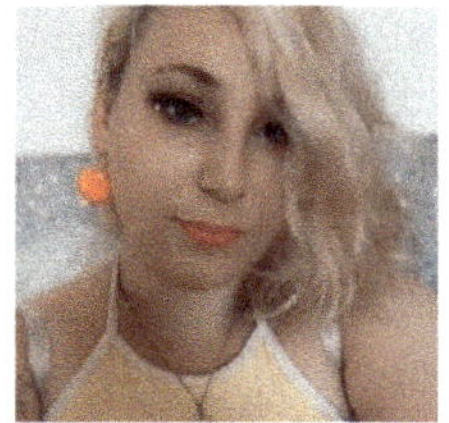

Eddie L. House is a 24 year-old genderqueer manic pixie daydream. They enjoy writing, roller skating, and getting very very drunk. Most likely to be found smoking out of a bedroom window or lying on the sofa complaining. You can find more of their work at Image Out Write, Anatolios, Hustling Verse, or tucked inside library books.

Kalandfitz is a young woman of color and first generation American who has had her battles with mental health. She volunteers with the Crisis Text Line, and wants to help advocate for mental health awareness in any way she can.

You can find more of her poetry on Instagram: @kalandfitz

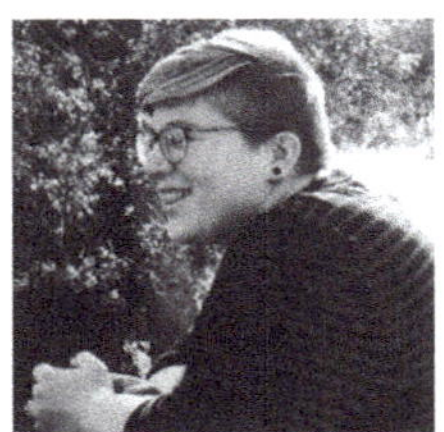

Kath Kane is an avid poet and aspiring author from Clinton, Massachusetts. She is currently pursuing a degree in Creative Writing with a concentration in poetry at Southern New Hampshire University. In her free time, she likes to perform at local poetry slams and express herself through painting and photography. She uses her social media platforms to share her work.

You can find Kath on Instagram: @kathkane_ or Facebook: @kathspoems

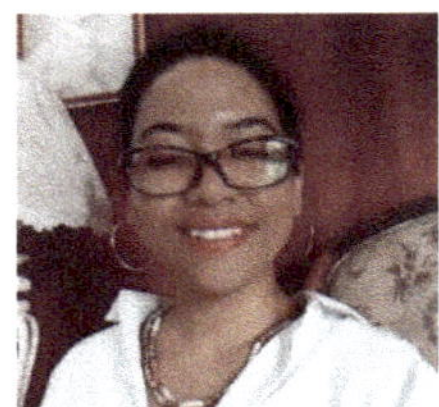

Born in a rural village within a forest in Sumatera, and now residing in Banjarbaru, South Kalimantan, Indonesia, **Naomi Karsudjono*** lives a simple life with her family. She enjoys painting, gardening, and sewing in the morning. Later in the night she pours her heart in words and share them with the world.

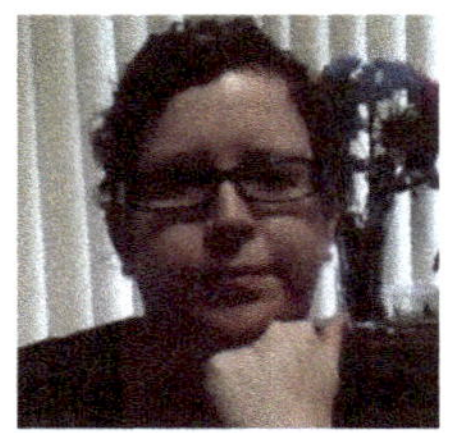

Suzanne Lea is a southern writer with a fondness for coffee, bare feet, and swear words. She's been published in several 'zines and journals, as well as the print anthologies - Crooked Letter i: Coming out in the South, published by New South Books and Love Notes You'll Never Read, from Gnashing Teeth Publishing. Her motto is, "Learn to forgive yourself for all the things you did to survive."

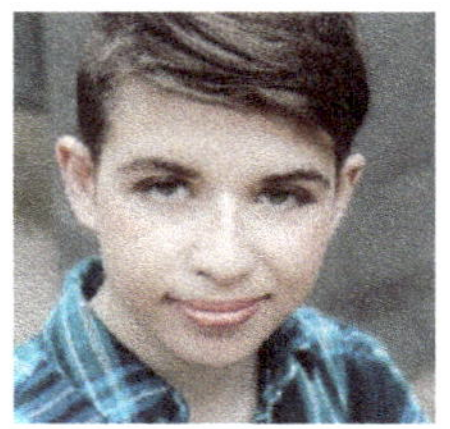

Polina Litvak is a writer, actor, and social service provider in the San Francisco Bay Area. Her poetry has previously been published in *The Distance of Skin: Poetry for the People in the Time of COVID-19* through City College of San Francisco. She enjoys singing along (badly) to cast recordings, buying books faster than she can read them, and texting cat pictures to her girlfriend.

Polina can be found on Twitter at @nerdfaerie and Instagram at @apolinariah.

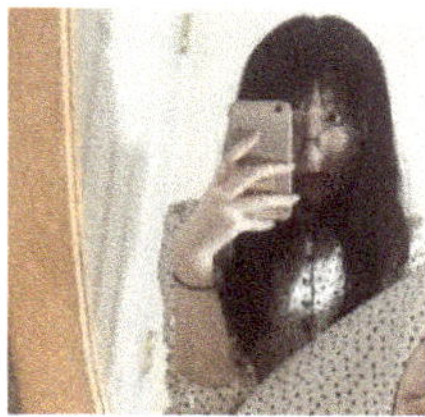

Angelina Luo is an 18-year-old college freshman. Her work focuses on visceral paintings of life as an Asian-American and a lesbian. She is often looking at pictures of frogs or drinking boba while reading.

You can find her work at @etchingsonthewall on Instagram.

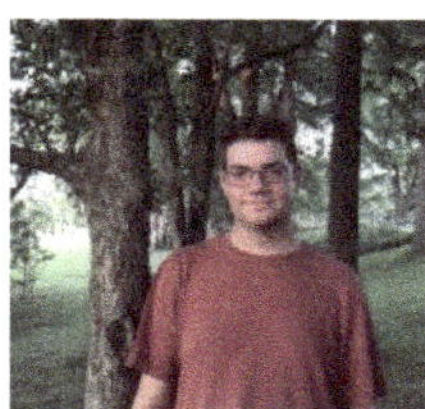

Nathaniel Luscombe* is a seventeen year-old Canadian who has never wanted to be anything but an author. When not writing, you can usually find him reading or exploring the art of writing. He also loves hanging out with the other ten people in his family, who have never been anything but supportive.

You can find Nathaniel on Instagram: @hecticreadinglife

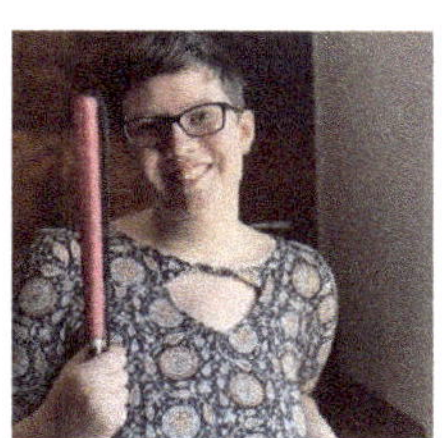

Amanda McCoy* is an author/illustrator and activist. Born visually impaired, later diagnosed with chronic illnesses, and a part of the LGBT+ community, Amanda enjoys creating artwork that empowers those who are different. After publishing her first picture book at 18, she engaged in public speaking in person and on TV, began creating artwork for nonprofits, and regularly updates a webcomic featuring a diverse cast!

You can find Amanda on Instagram and Facebook: @amandamccoyart

S. Rupsha Mitra is a 17 year-old student from India with a penchant for everything that is creative. She studies Psychology and is deeply interested in the theories of emotions and motivations. Passionate about art and poetry, she has co-founded a literary magazine with her friends.

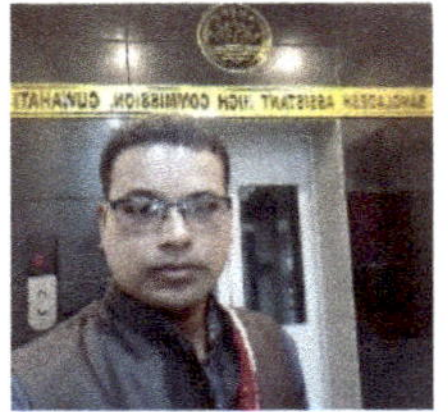

Guna Moran is an assamese poet and critic. His poems are being published in various international magazines, journals, webzines and anthologies. He lives in Assam, India.

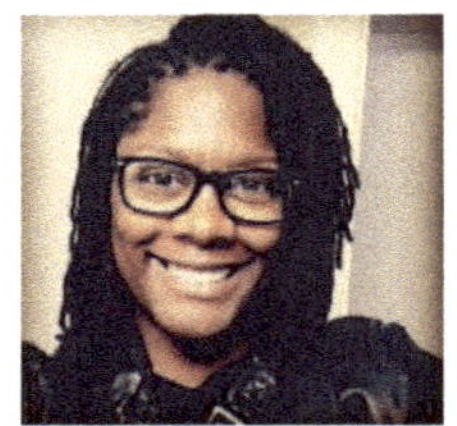

Karen R. Nelson* is a graduate student of the Creative Writing and Literary Arts program at University of Alaska Anchorage (UAA). Before starting her MFA, Karen served in and retired from the United States Air Force. Karen has published a nonfiction piece with the Alaska Women Speak Journal. She's also published two works in UNDERSTORY, an annual anthology of achievement at UAA. *You can track her eccentricities on her website, karenrnelson.com, on Twitter @thekrnelson, or on Instagram @thekrnelson.*

Ollie (**OJR**) is a non-binary teenage writer working through college to get their associate's degree. They like to make music, write stories, do art, and work with statistics.

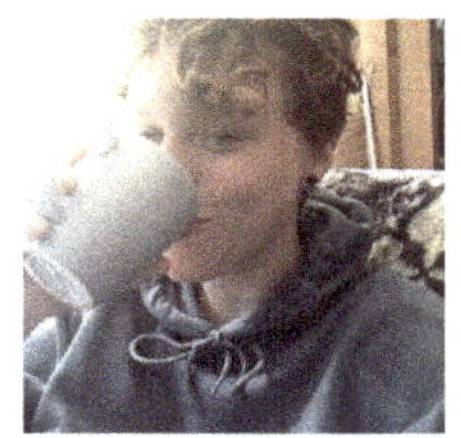

An absentee seminarian, **Theo Oliver** works in the social work field and spends their free time in music and in nature. Their biggest poetic inspirations are Mary Oliver, Andrea Gibson, and Shane Koyczan and their hope is to write with honesty, earnestness, and with especial attendance to the unexpectedly beautiful.

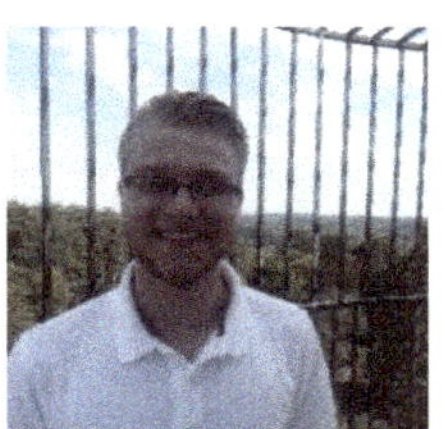

Erik Olson is a chemistry major in university. With his degree he hopes to pursue research in pharmaceuticals, specifically with allergies. Erik has dealt with anxiety and depression since fifth grade and continues to make strides every day. In his free time, he enjoys anything related to Star Trek, fishing, writing, and playing trumpet and piano.

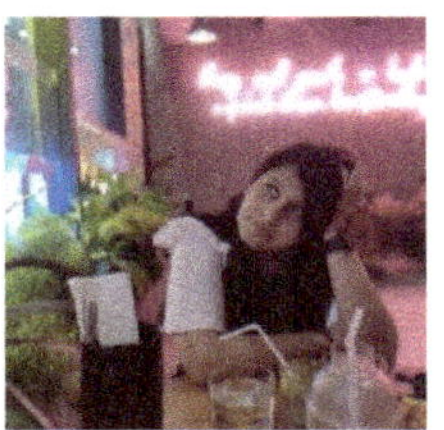

Somjeeta Pandey is currently working as an Assistant Professor of English at Gobardanga Hindu College, which is a government-aided college situated in West Bengal, India. She is also a part-time research scholar at the department of Humanities and Social Sciences, Indian Institute of Technology (IIT), Kharagpur.

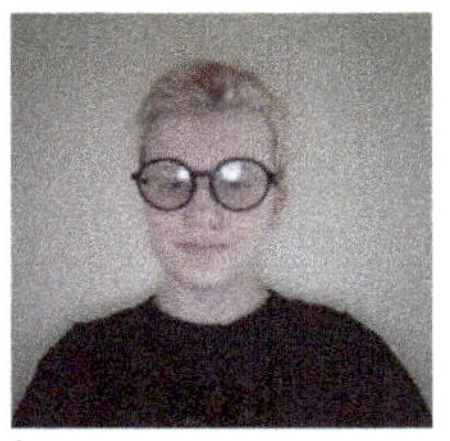

Frey Pokorny is a transgender man from the California bay area. He grew up in St. John's Portland Oregon, in a poor neighborhood, and has struggled with depression and anxiety disorder. His work focuses on the effects poverty has had on his mental health and his journey as a transgender man.

*You can find more of Frey on Instagram: @freypokorny_*

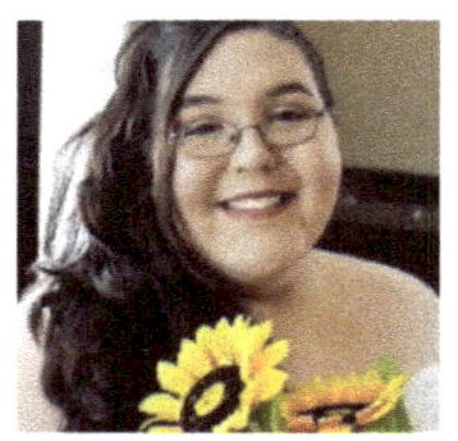

Kimmy Renee* is a free verse poet from Missouri, who started writing to help her cope, and finally had courage to post her words on Instagram. She uses her platform to bring awareness to mental health. While showing the reality of mental illness, Kimmy shows the light at the end of the tunnel.

In her free time, she does acrylic pour paintings and spoils her animals.

She has been published in the following: *There is Us Anthology*, *The Written Tales Magazine Volume II: Night Terrors*, and *HoneyFireLit Magazine Volume I: Memory Foam*.

You can read more of her work on Instagram @renee.kimmy

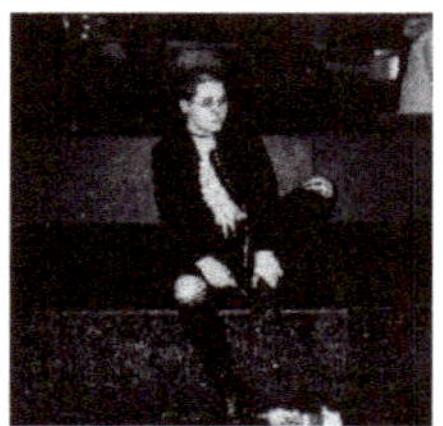

Naomi Slingerland* is a self-taught photographer originally from Medina, NY but now living in Albany, NY. They are 22 years old and have been taking pictures for over two years now. They love photographing things that most people would consider ugly and turning them into something beautiful.

You can find them on Instagram @some_sicc_pics

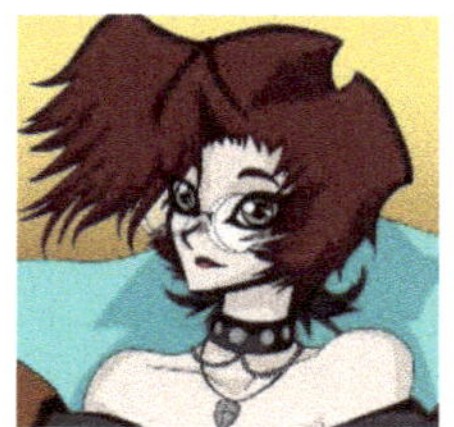

A storyboard artist from the middle of nowhere, **Stardust** possesses a maximum attachment to felines, obscure animated properties, and unnecessarily bright colors. Probably one of the strangest creatures to frequent the fellowship of the Church, she delights in exalting the beauty of Creation through story and art.

You can find her on Instagram @antelucanstardust or on Twitter as @AntelucanStarD.

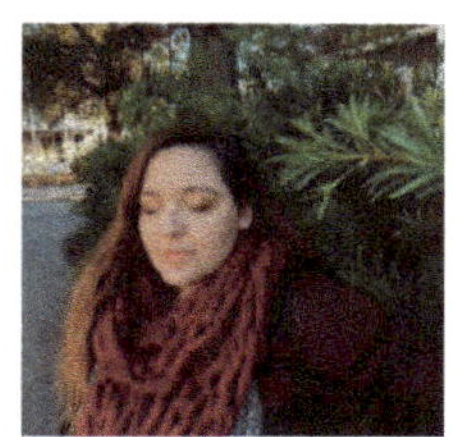

Stephanie Stone is 28 years-old and currently resides in South Korea. She is from the United States and was born and raised in North Carolina. Stephanie attended Appalachian State University where she received her bachelor's degree in 2014. In her spare time, Stephanie enjoys reading, playing with her golden retriever, listening to music, traveling, and writing poetry. She is dedicated and has a strong enthusiasm for adventure. Her first publication was "exhaustion-2020"

Rhea (R. Sunshine)* is a 21 -year-old trans woman from Wareham, Massachusetts. She's loved wordplay and writing stories ever since she was a little kid and transitioned more of her efforts into poetry 3 years ago. Her poetry has a focus on the exploration of gender identity, relationships, and aspects of human comfort.

Tiberius is an American transplant in Canada, who began life in Wisconsin but currently lives in Southern Ontario. He is inspired by people and has studied philosophy his entire life. He writes poems and stories that, hopefully, connect with that part of us that is constantly searching deeper shores.
You can find him on Instagram: @tiberius.the.scribe

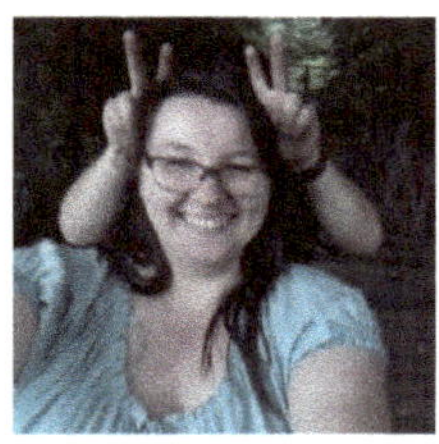

Martina Weiß was born in 1995 in Nördlingen (Germany). In secondary school, she was part of the school's newspaper, where she also "published" her very first original short story. She is now studying secondary school teaching at the University of Augsburg, where she is part of her university's Improvisational theater. If you tried to summarize Martina in one sentence, you would call her a crazy, childish, stubborn but tolerant dreamer.

She owns lots of dogs, is half Croatian, and hopes to publish her first book somewhere around 2021.

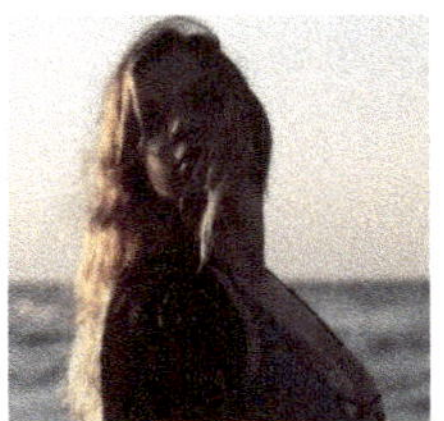

Noelle Weymouth finds beautiful things in beautiful places and has met the most beautiful people along the way. Her life has never been easy, and she has collected more scars than smiles along the way, but the numbers are finally starting to even out. She believes we all have scars in different places, and we all understand what it means to get them, but our wounds are just places to let the light in. She fought for her light and found herself through the eyes of a camera lens.

You can find her on Instagram (@nfwphotography_), Facebook (@NFWphoto), or on her website: https://nfwphotography.com

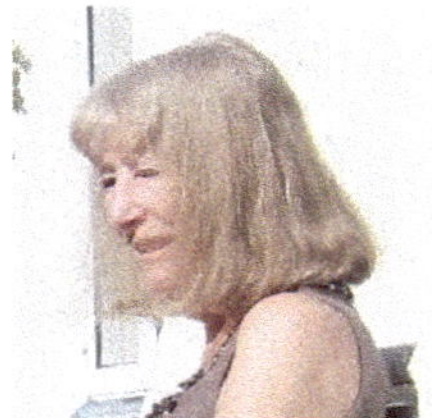

Lynn White lives in north Wales. Her work is influenced by issues of social justice and events, places and people she has known or imagined. She is especially interested in exploring the boundaries of dream, fantasy and reality. She was shortlisted in the Theatre Cloud 'War Poetry for Today' competition and has been nominated for a Pushcart Prize and a Rhysling Award. Her poetry has appeared in many publications including: Apogee, Firewords, Capsule Stories, Light Journal and So It Goes.

Find Lynn at lynnwhitepoetry.blogspot.com_and on Facebook: Lynn White Poetry

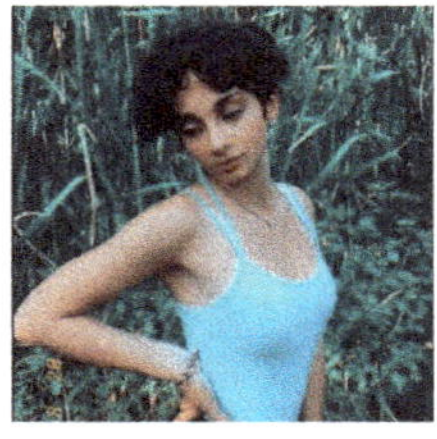

Clover Zicolella* is 19 years of age and resides in the state of Connecticut. Their works typically revolve around the psychology of Love, romance, and intimacy (platonic, romantic, and otherwise). They are not officially published, but write novels in their free time and hope to publish someday when they are finished. They love to write poetry and fiction, in varying genres. They are, however, a music major and hope to someday open their own record label.

You can find Clover's music at: soundcloud.com/devilish860

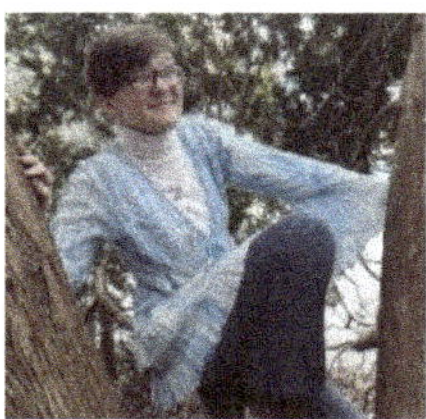

Ziel* is a creator. They really wish they could pick a more specific word, but the work that brings them joy ranges from poetry and playwriting to acrylic painting and sculpting, skipping through music and dance on the way. They find beauty in nearly everything, and feel an unending urge to make things better. Their favorite artist is Hozier, and they hope to one day handle fame with as much grace and humility. Until then, though, they will be satisfied if their work makes one person feel less alone in the world.

About the Editor:

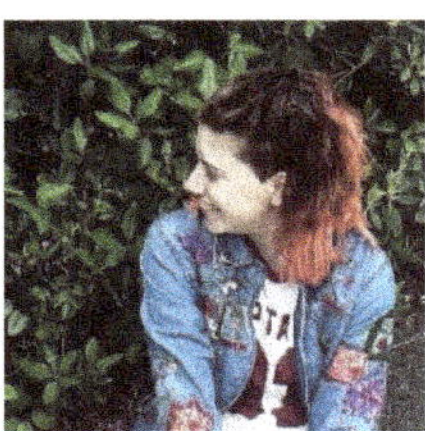

SJ Blasko* has been dreaming of making anthologies since middle school, and *There is Us* and *Faces to the Sun* have seen that dream come true. She is no stranger to mental health struggles, and much of her poetry revolves around her adolescent experiences with undiagnosed anxiety, depression, and severe PMDD, as well as chronic Lyme disease. March of 2021 will mark 2 years since she first went on anti-depressants, and those (together with the support of her friends) are helping her rediscover the bits of herself she lost to the darkness.

You can find her on Instagram @thesongsofsparrow, or check out her other books via Amazon and Goodreads.

Hungry for more? Check out these other works by talented Faces to the Sun contributors!

Poetry Collections and Chapbooks:
the flowers need love to grow too by SJ Blasko
Midnight Comes by SJ Blasko
Ode to Persephone by Riley Courtney
Erratic and Unnecessary by Erelah Emerson
Lost Lovers Series by Eddie L. House
Street Poems by Eddie L. House

Children's and Middle-Grade:
Grammy's Glasses by Maggie D. Brace
The Animal Adventures series by Sarah Hindmarsh
1001 Prompts series by Sarah Hindmarsh
Can I See? by Amanda McCoy
Jibbernocky: Books in Homes Special Charity Edition

Other Anthologies:
A Kind of Death from Uncommon Universes Press
Barrowby Scouts Fundraising Anthology from Creating with
   Kohla Publications
Bingeworthy from Havok Publishing
The Forgotten and The Fantastical (Vol. 2) from Mother's Milk
   Books
Nation from Barrio Blues Press
Stories That Sing from Havok Publishing
There Is Us from There is Us Anthologies
Warriors Against the Storm from Mt. Zion Ridge Press

Acknowledgements

Thank you so much to all the authors, artists, friends, and family who made this book possible, and especially a huge thank you to our Kickstarter backers:

AC Bennett
L.P. (for Katie Hanna)
G. Olson
Jack & Kathye Foster
Agatha
Megan Dere
Thomas B.
Backer #7
Alex McGilvery
Erelah E.
S. Stone (for Stephanie Stone)
Steven S.
Elyssa S. Schwendy
Hannah Rodes
Abi McCoy
Amanda Bolton
Doris D.

This book wouldn't be possible without you <3

There is Us was born from a desire to find a tangible way for small creators to help with COVID-19 relief efforts in the height of the pandemic.

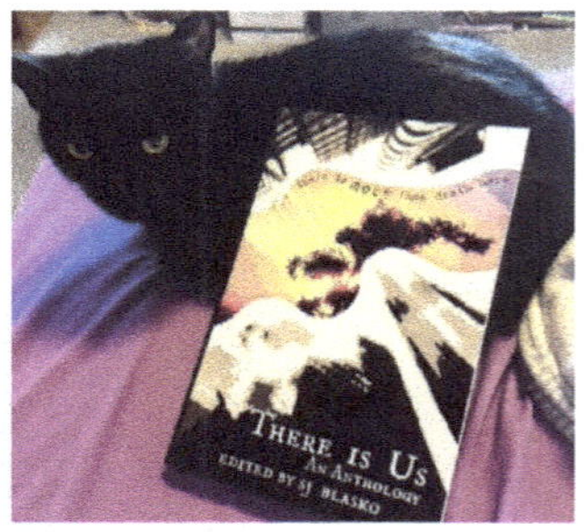

It operates using the stone soup principle — many hands make light work, and a little bit from everyone makes a beautiful thing.

The hope is that even while sales from this collection are going to organizations providing much-needed aid around the world, the pieces inside will uplift and soothe the souls of those trapped inside and longing for human connection.

You can find There is Us on Facebook and Instagram @there.is.us or purchase your copy through Amazon or payhip.com/b/kYW1

Thank you so much for supporting this project. <3

There is more than death here. There is us.

www.ingramcontent.com/pod-product-compliance
Lightning Source LLC
Chambersburg PA
CBHW052356030726

47599CB00014B/1090